COMPETING

ON

EXCELLENCE:

Healthcare Strategies for a Consumer-Driven Market

Alan M. Zuckerman and Russell C. Coile, Jr.

ACHE Management Series
Health Administration Press

Your board, staff, or clients may also benefit from this book's insight. For more information on quantity discounts, contact the Health Administration Press Marketing Manager at (312) 424-9470.

Library of Congress Cataloging-in-Publication Data

Zuckerman, Alan M.
    Competing on excellence : healthcare strategies for a consumer-driven market / by Alan M. Zuckerman and Russell C. Coile, Jr.
        p.   cm.
    Includes bibliographical references.
    ISBN 1-56793-210-X
    1. Health services administration.   2. Health facilities—Business management.   3. Total quality management.   I. Coile, Russell C.   II. Title.

RA971.Z788 2003
362.1'068—dc—21   2003047784

The paper used in this publication meets the minimum requirements of American National Standard for Information Sciences—Permanence of Paper for Printed Library Materials, ANSI Z39.48-1984. ∞™

Acquisitions editor: Audrey Kaufman; Project manager: Cami Cacciatore; Cover design: Matt Avery

Health Administration Press
A division of the Foundation of the
    American College of Healthcare Executives
1 North Franklin Street, Suite 1700
Chicago, IL 60606-4425
(312) 424-2800

COMPETING

ON

EXCELLENCE:

Healthcare Strategies for a Consumer-Driven Market

Contents

Foreword

COMPETING ON EXCELLENCE is the right message at the right time, by the right people, for the right audience. Historically, physicians almost exclusively determined where and how patient care would be delivered; over time, that decision-making power shifted to third-party payers such as insurance companies. Most recently, however, the American people have made it clear that they want to make those decisions themselves. And Americans are doing just that. Now considered consumers as well as patients, they are increasingly in control, making decisions about who will provide their care and which healthcare plan will best suit their needs. Moreover, they are willing to pay the extra cost that accompanies that decision making.

This shift of control has created a much different playing field for the contemporary healthcare organization. It is no longer enough to meet the needs of physicians and third-party payers. Meeting the needs of patients is more complex: It means successfully aligning the services of physicians, nurses, other staff, and even facilities, to serve, first and foremost, the patient. While successful healthcare organizations have focused on the needs of their patients for years, the new realities have altered the dimensions and scope of "excellence," "best in class," and "the gold standard." Even those successful organizations that were already recognized as patient centered have to rise to an even higher standard of care. We all have to do it better.

Fortunately, we have two experts to guide us on this new path to excellence. Alan Zuckerman is one of the leading healthcare strategic planners in the United States. He has worked with hundreds of organizations during his career. Not only is he an extraordinarily successful practitioner, he is a widely acclaimed author and presenter. Russ Coile, one of the leading healthcare futurists in the country, is a keen observer of healthcare trends, which allows him to adroitly forecast how the future will affect the journey we are now undertaking. Russ is also an accomplished and highly regarded author and presenter. Together they are the perfect combination to address the challenges before us.

Ultimately, this is a book about successful approaches and concrete suggestions, based on real-world examples, to understanding the future and acting effectively in the shifting patient care environment. The authors truly provide the reader with tools for "competing on excellence."

Thomas C. Dolan, Ph.D., FACHE, CAE
President and Chief Executive Officer
American College of Healthcare Executives

Preface

Competing on Excellence in a Consumer-Driven Market

> What defines excellence in a hospital? A business mind
> would look for lower expenses, higher revenues and prof-
> its, growing occupancy and improved productivity. Equally
> important in light of recent headlines about patient safety
> would be quality of care as measured by mortality and
> complication rates . . . These institutions are characterized
> by superior management and a focus on continuous
> improvement.
>
> —*Richard Service (2000)*

IT IS A new day for healthcare consumers, hospitals, and physicians. Report card rankings on healthcare providers are public and easily accessible on the Internet. An increasing body of evidence shows that best practices produce higher quality at lower cost (Lippman 2002). But how and where do consumers get the information on which hospitals and physicians have the best outcomes? Healthcare's report card movement is gaining momentum, despite limited enthusiasm or cooperation from providers. Employers, consumer groups, nonprofit foundations, commercial firms, government agencies, and the media are joining the fray. Whereas the early rankings featured academic medical centers, new sources of report card data have broadened the ratings to include nearly every hospital over 50 beds. Let the competition begin!

We wrote *Competing on Excellence* to provide a management guide to this new marketplace. As a market forecaster (Coile) and a strategist (Zuckerman), we believe the healthcare market has completely flipped in the past five years. The arrival of report cards, 10,000 health-related web sites, and informed consumers signal the end of an era—managed care— and the arrival of a new environment for healthcare—consumer choice. Thanks to the explosion of Internet-based information, Harvard Business School professor Regina Herzlinger's scenario of empowered consumers making economic choices can now be played out. She argues, "Let's put consumers in charge of healthcare" (Herzlinger 2002). And why not? Managed care and government are ineffective in slowing the rise in health costs or improving the quality of services.

The basis for competition in the 1990s was wholesale transactions between large integrated delivery systems with Ian Morrison's "large, ugly buyers"—the consolidated health insurers (Morrison 2000). Today, providers and plans are competing in a retail medicine marketplace in which the patient, not the health plan, is the real customer. In the post–managed care marketplace, hospitals and doctors can make their market by demonstrating excellence in clinical outcomes and customer service.

SEARCHING FOR EXCELLENCE REVEALS THE CORE CONCEPTS

When we began thinking about this book, the initial focus was on centers of excellence, an update of service-line strategies in the fresh context of a retail medicine–style of competition. However, when our colleagues were quick to remind us that the centers concept was really "new wine in old bottles," our focus on excellence broadened.

Some of the best books on corporate excellence have been published in the past decade, including Jim Collins and Jerry Porras's *Built to Last* (1994), Leonard Berry's *Discovering the Soul of Service* (1999), and Collins's recent work, *Good to Great* (2001), based on comparisons of similar companies in the same industries. We revisited Tom Peters and Bob Waterman's *In Search of Excellence* (1982), which had catapulted the concept of corporate excellence to the forefront of management thinking. Several of Peters and Waterman's observations are still relevant today and highly instructive to healthcare organizations.

Many of the nation's leading management consultants have pursued the elusive concept of corporate excellence. In the search, the experts have used numerous criteria to define an excellent company as the following:

- Consistently profitable
- Successful across boom and bust business cycles
- In the top ranks of respect by its customers
- Pursued (and imitated) by competitors
- Continually innovative with new products and services
- Having strong employee esprit and morale

Among leading experts, the concept of value-driven leadership anchors all other elements of creating and sustaining corporate excellence. What Peters and Waterman refer to as shared values are similar to Berry's value-driven leadership, which ties in with Collins's level 5 leadership. The books of these authors have different orientations—innovation, sustained success, and customer service—yet offer similarities in the advice they share with managers.

- *Structure* should be simple and highly flexible.
- *Systems* enable consistent achievement of execution despite changes in personnel or business cycles.
- *Style* is a reflection of corporate culture, in which trust-based relationships, generosity, and a culture of discipline are important.
- *Staff* is the foundation of all enterprises, taking priority ("first who, then what"), and management invests in employee excellence.
- *Skills* enable a company to control its destiny and use technology as an accelerator to create new products.
- *Strategy* is the combination of strategic focus, brand cultivation, and a willingness to confront brutal facts without losing faith.

Collins comments in *Built to Last* that he feels a bit like Dorothy in *The Wizard of Oz*, who, after her long search for the wizard, pulls back the curtain and discovers the supernatural being to be just human. Collins observes: "Those who build visionary companies are not necessarily more brilliant, more charismatic, more creative, more complex thinkers, more adept at coming up with great ideas . . . The builders of visionary companies tend to be simple, even simplistic, in their approach to business" (Collins 2001). Companies that have enjoyed long-term success are social institutions— individuals working together in a common cause. Building a visionary company is a combination of a core ideology (core values and core purpose) and an envisioned future (10- to 30-year "big hairy audacious goals").

ORGANIZATION OF THE BOOK

The chapters of *Competing on Excellence* are designed to be read and enjoyed by our readers in whatever order they believe is of greatest interest. Our suggestion is to start by reading the opening and closing chapters. They are theoretical bookends for the content in the intervening chapters that are more detailed and practical. Chapters 1 and 10 provide the argument for competing on excellence and outline the essential process of creating a culture of excellence. A brief listing of topics for each chapter is outlined below.

CHAPTER 1
COMPETING ON EXCELLENCE: THE NEW BASIS OF HEALTHCARE STRATEGY

- Defining excellence from the perspective of customers, payers, and physicians
- Developing and differentiating an intangible product
- Achieving superior clinical quality outcomes
- Creating excellent clinical care: the role of teaching and research
- Excelling in customer service (and having highly satisfied patients)

CHAPTER 2
POSITIONING IN A CONSUMER-DRIVEN ENVIRONMENT

- Commercial sources of ratings and rankings
- Nonprofit and consumer organizations
- Employer groups
- Government report cards
- The ratings game
- The new consumers
- Customer segmentation and differentiation strategies

CHAPTER 3
MARKET STRATEGIES FOR REVENUE GROWTH

- Increasing market share
- Expanding service areas, domain, and turf
- Filling gaps in the continuum of services
- Developing niche services
- Repackaging existing services for targeted marketing

CHAPTER 4
BUSINESS DEVELOPMENT AND PROGRAM PLANNING

- Developing an effective business plan
- Maximizing the value of the business plan
- Choosing contents of a typical business plan
- Developing an effective business plan
- Planning for start-up, roll-out, and operations
- Fostering entrepreneurialism and leadership

CHAPTER 5
HEALTHCARE'S SERVICE-LINE MANAGEMENT REVIVAL

- Lessons from the private sector on product-line management
- Alternatives for management organization
- System versus local management challenges and approaches
- Implications for enterprisewide management

CHAPTER 6
FROM REDUCING MEDICAL ERRORS TO REAL QUALITY IMPROVEMENT

- Improving efficiency, reducing costs
- Profiling performance, reducing errors
- Ensuring best-of-class outcomes
- Benchmarking

CHAPTER 7
PHYSICIAN STRATEGIES

- Fostering a culture of physician entrepreneurship
- Managing physicians and ensuring financial accountability
- Recruiting "top docs"
- Creating alliances with "branded" academic centers
- Building a base of physician referrals
- Building relationships with key physician groups

CHAPTER 8
WORLD-CLASS SERVICE

- Adhering to customer-defined service expectations
- Monitoring and measuring customer satisfaction
- Building a culture of service
- Creating service recovery strategies
- Marketing, differentiation, and positioning by patient satisfaction

CHAPTER 9
COMPETING BY DESIGN

- Using evidence-based design
- Creating healing environments
- Reducing sources of stress in patient care environments
- Creating positive distractions
- Offering alternative medicine

CHAPTER 10
CULTURE OF EXCELLENCE
- Creating a culture of entrepreneurship and intrapreneurship
- Measuring success: market share, financial performance, outcomes, and preference ratings
- Evaluating progress and adjusting as required
- Maintaining the vision and keeping the flame alive
- Taking excellence to the next level: lessons for the future

WHY THIS BOOK IS TIMELY AND IMPORTANT

We believe that competing on excellence will be the new basis for competition and strategy for American healthcare organizations in the decade ahead. The threat of collapse of managed care has created an opportunity for a new scenario to unfold, featuring the informed consumer. Shifting gears from a wholesale, managed care market to a retail-oriented, consumer-led market may take some doing. Large integrated delivery systems were built for strength and market leverage, not nimble market competition for consumers. This 180-degree change in strategy will not be achieved overnight, but change is possible. We are inspired by the growing numbers of healthcare institutions that have achieved ratings like top 100, five-star, magnet hospitals, and the 100 best places to work in America.

Jim Collins reminds us that "going from good to great is not easy, and that not every organization will successfully make the shift. By definition, it is not possible for everyone to be above average" (Collins 2001). Yet Collins does assert that those who strive to turn good into great will find the process no more painful or exhausting than those who settle for just letting things "wallow in mind-numbing mediocrity." In our view, the search for excellence is a journey, not a destination. Hospitals that have achieved the 90th percentile of patient satisfaction will set their sights higher, on achieving the 95th percentile. That is how good becomes great.

Healthcare is a unique economic sector that in the past has only imperfectly resembled a true market with buyers, sellers, and economic rationality. That is changing. The discipline of market competition can go far to improve efficiency and promote effectiveness, driving down costs and reducing the intrusion of third parties in the provider-patient relationship. The term "excellence" has many strategic implications for improving the quality of health outcomes, designing facilities for healing, ensuring patient safety, and raising customer service levels that are at the very heart of what motivated us to undertake this project in the first place.

Every hospital, health system, and physician organization can strive for greatness. *Competing on Excellence* is about the search for meaning in American healthcare, or more precisely, the search for excellence in healthcare that is meaningful for its providers, patients, and public.

REFERENCES

Berry, L. L. 1999. *Discovering the Soul of Service: The Nine Drivers of Sustainable Business Success.* New York: Free Press.

Collins, J. 2001. *Good to Great: Why Some Companies Make the Leap and Others Don't.* New York: HarperBusiness.

Collins, J. C., and J. I. Porras. 1994. *Build to Last: Successful Habits of Visionary Companies.* New York: HarperBusiness.

Herzlinger, R. E. 2002. "Let's Put Consumers in Charge of Health Care." *Harvard Business Review* 80 (7): 44–55.

Lippman, H. 2002. "Front and Center: Defining Excellence in Specialized Care." *Business & Health* June 3. [Online article; retrieved 8/5/02.] http://www.businessandhealth.com.

Morrison, I. 2000. *Health Care in the New Millennium.* San Francisco: Jossey-Bass.

Peters, T. J., and R. H. Waterman, Jr. 1982. *In Search of Excellence: Lessons From America's Best Run Companies.* New York: Harper & Row.

Service, R. 2000. "The Top 100 Hospitals." *Business & Health* February 1. [Online article; retrieved 11/8/02.] http://www.businessandhealth.com.

Acknowledgments

THE IDEA FOR this project began to take shape in the midst of writing Alan's last book, *Improve Your Competitive Strategy: A Guide for the Healthcare Executive*. Differentiation on the basis of quality was emerging as a major competitive battleground, driven by the increasing availability of information on quality and the efforts by many healthcare organizations to develop centers of excellence to distinguish themselves from their competitors. However, it proved difficult to get this new project off the ground. The original idea for the book was to use the centers-of-excellence theme as the focal point. However, that idea failed to gel and the project stalled.

Enter Russ Coile. Russ was both enthusiastic about the concept and able to reformulate it and repackage it in a most exciting way. We agreed to collaborate on the development of the manuscript and the ball really started rolling. Without Russ' energy and drive, which incidentally resulted in developing a first draft in record time, this idea may never have taken flight.

Like most projects, many contributed both formally and informally. First of all, we would like to thank our clients, who were responsible for the overwhelming majority of the concepts we developed in this book and some of the specific case study material. We hope that when you read this book, it provides some insight and assistance and, thus, a positive return on investment for your contribution.

Second, we owe a debt of gratitude to our staffs. Some suffered through seemingly endless diatribes about this or that concept, others made a suggestion or two (or more) for improvement, while a few labored greatly to make sure the results made sense. In the latter category, we thank Susan Arnold, Christine Passaglia, and Debbie Sullivan in particular.

Last, but not least, there are, of course, our families. While both our wives might argue that if we hadn't been involved in this project we would have wasted the time playing golf (and there's at least some truth in that), it's highly likely that at least some of the time was "stolen" from them as well as our teenage children. Although the teenagers are too cool to care, we do appreciate your collective indulgence of all our extracurricular activities, including this one.

Alan M. Zuckerman   Russell C. Coile, Jr.
Philadelphia, Pennsylvania   Washington, Texas

Chapter 1

Competing on Excellence: The New Basis of Healthcare Strategy

> Although [excellent] companies are strong performers, profit itself is not a defining value; rather it is an outcome. The pursuit of excellence, however, is a defining value. The word good is rarely used in [excellent] companies. The pride of achievement comes from striving for excellence. Sustainable success stems from insisting on exceptionally high standards in operating the business . . . The quest for excellence creates economic value, but is valuable in its own right for it uplifts the human spirit and burnishes the joy of personal achievement. Excellence is worthwhile even if only the gods can see it, and this is its true meaning.
>
> *—Leonard L. Berry (1999)*

COMPETING ON EXCELLENCE is the challenge and the opportunity for market leadership by twenty-first century healthcare organizations. This is the age of "accountable consumerism" (Vinn 2000). In today's consumer-choice marketplace, excellence is defined by consumers in terms they understand, like service, responsiveness, communication, caring, access, convenience, cleanliness, wayfinding, and, importantly, parking! The shift from managed care (wholesale model) to a consumer-driven (retail model) market was predicted by Regina Herzlinger (1997), who foresaw that managed care was caving in to consumer desires for wide-open access and free choice of providers. Herzlinger's ideas about consumer empowerment could become a national movement if large numbers of employers shift from defined-benefit to defined-contribution strategies and give employees the cash to purchase health plans and services.

If you or a loved one is ill, you want the best care in the best health facility. Now health consumers can go virtually anywhere in their market, or in the United States, for a nominal deductible. Excellence matters in the healthcare market when consumers have choice and the ability to gain access to best-of-the-best hospitals and physicians. In an ideal market, consumers have choice, access, and information. The Internet has created the informed consumer, who has access to more than 10,000 health-related web sites for health advice and information. More than 120 million Americans are online regularly, and half of them are "health-seekers" who access health information at least monthly, according to the Pew Foundation's "Internet and American Life Project" in Washington, DC (Fox and Rainie 2002).

The availability of report cards that grade hospitals and health plans gives consumers an ability to compare five-star hospitals and find the top 100 hospitals in the United States. Yale–New Haven Hospital recently trumpeted a ratings trifecta, being selected as one of *U.S. News & World Report*'s "best hospitals," receiving an award from the American Hospital Association as one of the 100 "Most Wired" healthcare institutions, and having nine Yale–New Haven surgeons recognized in *New York Magazine*'s top 100 minimally invasive surgeons in the tristate region (D'Antonio 2002a, 2002b; Peart 2002).

The takeaway lesson: in the market-share battle based on excellence, the competition is regional, statewide, and national. Every local hospital with a heart program or cancer center is now competing with Johns Hopkins Hospital and Health System, the Mayo Clinic, and M.D. Anderson Cancer Center. That is the *challenge*—competing with out-of-area centers of excellence that exert a magnet pull on local consumers. The *opportunity* is to take share and patients away from regional centers by convincing consumers that hometown healthcare is equal to or better than care in distant medical centers where patients would be isolated from friends and family members. Patients can log onto www.healthgrades.com and compare their local hospital with regional and national competitors. Earning five stars—and the bragging rights that come with that rating—can catapult a hometown health facility to major league status.

IN A CONSUMER-CHOICE MARKET, PATIENTS CAN CHOOSE THE BEST OF THE BEST

Hello, Dr. Welby! It's like the 1950s again. Consumers can go to virtually any doctor or hospital of their choice. Managed care's increasing abandonment of gatekeepers and prior authorization has opened a floodgate of demand that is propelling higher volumes of hospital admissions, surgeries, and emergency department visits across the nation. At the same time, managed care has been forced to retreat from exclusive provider agreements that steered patients to preferred hospitals but prevented access to others. Some hospitals and doctors have successfully refused to sign health maintenance organization (HMO) contracts until they receive rate increases. The tough tactics are working, with many providers gaining higher fee schedules. Recent efforts by some California HMOs to create tiers of providers with higher consumer copaymentss quickly generated a wave of criticism, and the HMOs have pulled back.

HMOs and health insurers are weighing their next moves to hold down costs. They have two alternatives: (1) channel patients to cost-effective, high-quality centers of excellence or (2) keep increasing consumer deductibles and copayments that discourage patients from using out-of-network health providers. Minnesota's Blue Cross organization recently criticized widespread hospital construction as a "medical arms race" that would inflate insurance premiums. Providers fought back, charging that Blue Cross and Blue Shield of Minnesota had contributed to the building boom when the Blues plan engaged in a $90 million joint venture to construct a 74-bed facility with a clinic in Fargo, North Dakota, where two community facilities already existed (Benko 2002). In neighboring Wisconsin, state legislators defeated a proposal that would have banned all hospital construction, and at the time of this writing, the legislature is still considering whether to reinstate certificate-of-need review for future construction projects. Competing on excellence—in-state-of-the-art medical equipment, new facilities, and information—could become more difficult if states revive capital expenditure review or certificate-of-need regulations.

THE TOP 100 HOSPITALS IN AMERICA

Solucient, a market research organization, recognizes an elite group of hospitals—the "top 100"—each year. Solucient maintains an extensive national database of Medicare cost reports, as well as information on managed care, pharmaceutical utilization, and other health industry data. For a decade, Solucient's annual ratings have identified those hospitals whose cost and quality performance is the best in the nation. The rankings are based on eight performance measures: risk-adjusted mortality index; risk-adjusted complications index; severity-adjusted average length of stay; expense per adjusted discharge (case mix and wage-adjusted); profitability (cash flow margin); proportion of outpatient revenue; productivity (total asset turnover ratio); and data quality. Hospitals are grouped into five comparison groups:

1. Major teaching hospitals (determined by number of acute-care beds, intern-/resident-per-bed ratio, and sponsorship or involvement in graduate medical education programs)
2. Teaching hospitals (determined by number of acute-care beds, intern-/resident-per-bed ratio, and sponsorship or involvement in graduate medical education programs)
3. Small community hospitals (25 to 99 acute-care beds)
4. Medium community hospitals (100 to 249 acute-care beds)
5. Large community hospitals (250 or more acute-care beds)

Solucient's 100 top hospitals are performance leaders in their communities—consistently providing better outcomes and demonstrating increasing efficiency. Table 1.1 shows a five-year comparison of Solucient's 100 top hospitals' benchmark performance compared with all peer hospitals.

If every hospital performed with the same level of efficiency and effectiveness as Solucient's top 100, healthcare expenses would decline by an aggregate $8.9 billion per year. Americans would be healthier if every hospital has outcomes like the top 100. The annual number of complications would be reduced by nearly 67,000, and an additional 66,000 patients could survive (Solucient 2003).

Solucient gives special recognition to an elite group of hospitals that are the most consistent winners of the 100 Top Hospitals: Benchmarks for Success award. Solucient and academic researchers will be studying these consistently high-performing organizations to learn more about their management, clinical, and governance practices (Solucient 2003).

Solucient has launched additional recognition programs for specialized service units, and additional centers-of-excellence ratings may be offered in the future. Each category has its own criteria. Cardiovascular ratings, for example, are based on factors such as acute myocardial infarction mortality, coronary arterial bypass graft (CABG) mortality, percent of coronary angioplasty patients who required CABG during their stay, as well as severity- and wage-adjusted cost per discharge and severity-adjusted length of stay (Solucient 2001). Solucient rankings for large teaching hospitals generally mirror the *U.S. News & World Report*'s "Best Hospitals in America." The Cleveland Clinic has been rated the number one cardiac care program in the United States by *U.S. News & World Report* from among the Council of Teaching Hospitals and has also been ranked among Solucient's best cardiovascular centers. Top 100 rankings

Table 1.1 Five-Year Copmparison of Solucient's 100 Top Hospitals' Benchmark Performance Compared with All Peer Hospitals

	2000		1999		1998		1997		1996	
	Benchmark	Peer	Benchmark	Peer	Benchmark	Peer	Benchmark	Peer	Benchmark	Peer
Medicare case mix index	1.4794	1.2451	1.4317	1.2564	1.5169	1.2623	1.4924	1.2849	1.5036	1.2807
Survival rate (%), unadjusted	96.05	95.70	95.40	95.04	95.61	95.34	95.57	95.25	95.59	95.11
Average length of stay (days)	3.80	4.10	4.12	4.44	4.25	4.52	4.18	4.47	4.15	4.44
Salary and benefits per FTE personnel ($)	42,972	40,988	41,963	39,078	40,517	38,222	39,750	37,376	38,222	36,358
FTEs per adjusted average daily census	4.96	5.09	4.94	5.24	5.11	5.28	4.95	5.27	5.09	5.23
Expenses per adjusted discharge, case mix and wage adjusted ($)	3,704	4,532	3,509	4,365	3,452	4,249	3,509	4,126	3,530	3,998
Cash flow margin (%)	15.39	9.16	16.44	9.49	16.93	10.47	16.30	11.92	18.44	12.00
Total profit margin (%)	6.60	1.45	8.71	1.88	10.54	4.04	9.48	5.34	11.77	5.06
Total asset turnover ratio	1.04	0.92	1.09	0.91	1.08	0.925	1.04	0.94	1.13	0.96
Current ratio	2.30	2.15	2.23	2.13	2.13	2.05	1.91	2.08	2.06	2.05

Continued

Table 1.1 *Continued*

	2000		1999		1998		1997		1996	
	Benchmark	Peer	Benchmark	Peer	Benchmark	Peer	Benchmark	Peer	Benchmark	Peer
Special care days, as a percentage of all acute days ($)	12.66	10.55	12.32	10.45	11.98	10.10	11.23	8.19	10.72	7.75
Admissions per bed	51.78	41.64	51.50	40.80	53.59	38.86	50.25	38.34	47.45	37.28
FTEs per 100 adjusted discharges, case mix and wage adjusted	3.59	4.46	3.73	4.94	3.73	5.08	4.10	5.06	4.15	5.17
Overhead expense as percentage of operating expense (%)	32.74	31.49	32.54	31.70	30.79	31.81	31.91	31.99	33.33	32.73

Note: FTE = full-time equivalent.
Source: Solucient. 2003. *Solucient Top 100 Hospitals,* 17. Evanston, IL: Solucient.

are now published by Solucient for cardiovascular, clinical research, intensive care units, and orthopedics.

Solucient has already documented some of the performance differences demonstrated by the best of their top 100 hospitals. The top-flight hospitals achieve higher survival rates and fewer patient complications at lower costs. Patients at hospitals that won Solucient's 100 Top Hospitals award four or more times were 21 percent less likely to have postoperative respiratory complications (Solucient 2003).

In addition to superior quality, benchmark hospitals in the top 100 also achieve more successful outcomes with fewer resources. These hospitals treat more patients and demonstrate greater usage of special care units, yet use fewer employees at lower costs. In 2000, Solucient's top 100 hospitals' adjusted expenses were 18 percent lower than their peers. Both cash flow margin and total profit margin have also remained remarkably high. In 2000, Solucient's 100 top benchmark hospitals achieved a median total profit margin of 8.81 percent, more than 5 percentage points higher than the median for the peers (Solucient 2003).

INCENTIVES FOR EXCELLENCE

More rewards may exist for excellence than just public recognition and dominant market share. Financial incentives are beginning to be offered by health plans and employers to hospitals and medical groups whose performance exceeds benchmark standards. In Philadelphia, Independence Blue Cross (IBC) has launched a high-visibility program to reward hospitals for quality (George 2002). IBC senior officials are convinced that high-quality care is less expensive care, with fewer complications, shorter stays, and better outcomes. The Blues plan is backing its commitment to quality with a promise to give hospitals additional reimbursement if the providers achieve quality goals. IBC will use existing quality tools and measures, including some from the Leapfrog Group in Washington, DC, as well as the database of the Pennsylvania Health Care Cost Containment Commission. Specific targets are being negotiated in long-term contracts between IBC and local providers in the Philadelphia area, including Mercy Health and Chestnut Hill HealthCare.

The Philadelphia initiative is one of a handful of incentive compensation arrangements to reward quality by other insurers, including Empire Blue Cross Blue Shield in New York. Excellent physicians may share rewards when their medical groups exceed target goals set by HMOs or employer groups. Dr. Norman Vinn, vice president for the Call Doctor

Company, predicts: "As patients shoulder a larger share of their own healthcare costs, they'll expect more from physicians—and reward those who meet expectations" (Vinn 2000). The Pacific Business Group on Health has experimented with bonuses for medical groups that exceeded its targets for health promotion based on Health Plan Employer Data and Information Set data. Pacific Business Group's efforts have met with mixed responses from California physicians. Dr. Steve Carson, a quality consultant based at the University of California, San Diego, warned employers and HMOs that "doctors would not respond well to bonuses which are actually withholds from the physician fee" (Carson 2002). Until the Pacific Business Group establishes targets for quality, many will consider this approach a waste of time.

STRATEGIES FOR COMPETING ON EXCELLENCE

What makes a "good" company "great"? Management consultant Jim Collins debunks a number of myths about excellence in his book, *Good to Great* (Collins 2001). Charismatic leaders make great headlines, but they do not always make great profits. Leaders who were brilliant in growth cycles of the economy are not always able to reposition their companies when business conditions become turbulent. The good news is that innovative organizations in every sector of the economy are demonstrating the enduring qualities, lasting values, and sustainable strategies that healthcare organizations can use to compete on excellence.

That Vision Thing

A compelling vision of a future achievement can motivate fundamental change in an organization. Jim Collins and Jerry Porras (1994) call them "BHAG"s—big, hairy, audacious goals. These are goals that will take years to achieve. Putting a man on the moon was, by definition, a BHAG, as was Boeing's development of the 747 airplane. In the health field, the Celera Corporation's decision to beat the world's biotechnology scientists to decipher the genomic code was astonishing in its boldness. Celera developed high-capability gene decoding devices that allowed them to leapfrog the competition and beat their rivals' goals by three years. Chicago's Northwestern Memorial Hospital predicted in the early 1990s that managed care would never dominate Chicagoland and disbanded its eight-hospital managed care network. Instead, the hospital undertook a rebuilding project to rival the construction of the pyramids, spending

$580 million on a 500-bed replacement hospital designed with a patient-centered-care model. The new Northwestern facility is a home run, operating profitably and at high levels of occupancy.

Great Boards

Great organizations need great boards. As the experiences of Enron, Tyco, and WorldCom demonstrate, great companies are not directed by a board composed of high-profile executives who jet in for four-hour board meetings. Boards of great companies recognize their obligation is to their share-*holders,* who have invested in the company for the long term, not the share*flippers,* who may hold a majority of the company's stock but are in it only for short-term gains. In healthcare, the collapse of Allegheny Health, Education and Research Foundation (AHERF) in Philadelphia and Pittsburgh led to the breakup of one of the nation's best-known integrated delivery systems. There appears to be no doubt that the AHERF board and senior executives were directly responsible for the system's failure that led to bankruptcy and the jailing of its former chief executive officer.

Centers of Excellence

U.S. News & World Report's annual "Best Hospitals in America" designation was not the first program of recognition for the best in medicine. The concept of centers of excellence dates back to the 1960s when the federal government began to recognize medical centers with superior programs in heart, cancer, stroke, and other diseases. These teaching hospitals and academic medical centers were selected based on their research capabilities and exceptional clinical outcomes. The federally backed concept of regionalization sought to channel patients to a limited number of high-quality medical centers where clinical outcomes were superior.

Federal funding for comprehensive health planning established a national network of health systems agencies in the 1970s to promote regionalization, and many states gave these agencies certificate-of-need controls over capital expenditures to prevent high spending on facilities and equipment among competing hospitals. Almost a dozen states still continue some form of certificate-of-need controls over new facilities or capital expenditures, and more are calling to install certificates of need. The theory behind certificates of need is, in part, that tertiary and quaternary services—around which centers of excellence are often structured—need to be rationed (i.e., through good regulation) to maintain high quality and keep duplication to a minimum. Centers of excellence are popular with consumers and could become vehicles for select procedure contracting with insurers or employers in the future.

Great People

A nurturing climate for its workforce is one of the hallmarks of excellent organizations, as cited by Peters and Waterman (1982), Collins (2001), Berry (1999), and many of the best minds in management consulting. A high-performance workforce is the result of a priority investment in skill building as well as the willingness by top management to allow its employees to make autonomous decisions. Workers who believe in the goals and values of the organization enjoy greater job satisfaction and demonstrate it with higher productivity. Workers recognize the authenticity of values, like putting patients first, if they are matched by a commitment from top management. The "star" quality of top physicians is increasingly a magnet for consumer self-referrals as well as traditional doctor-to-doctor channels.

In Chapel Hill, the University of North Carolina (UNC) took pride in a recent announcement that 46 UNC physicians had been listed as "best doctors" in the state by the *Business North Carolina* magazine (Hughes 2002). For nursing, the American Nurses Magnet Association's Recognition Program, is a visible symbol of nursing excellence in nearly 60 hospitals across the nation. Creating a patient-centered facility in the rebuilding of Chicago's Northwestern Memorial Hospital had another benefit—the hospital has been recognized as one of the "100 Best Places to Work" by *Working Mothers* magazine (2003).

Superior Service

Healthcare providers are recognizing the importance of pleasing patients. As the report card movement gains momentum across the country, a number of states, consumer groups, and nonprofit foundations are focusing on patient satisfaction as a prime indicator of provider performance. Report cards in California, Maryland, New York, Rhode Island, and southeast Michigan rely primarily on patient satisfaction for their hospital ratings. As one California primary care physician notes: "Healthcare has, for many years, been in denial about its status as a service industry. It has been much more of a technology industry with highly erratic levels of customer service. Healthcare must evolve into a true service industry" (Vinn 2000).

Hospitals are required to monitor patient satisfaction by the Joint Commission on Accreditation of Healthcare Organizations (Joint Commission) and to demonstrate they have acted in response to consumer complaints. Service management consultant Gail Scott (2001a), advises that "feedback will drive improvement if it is about celebrating good work done or focuses on course correction." Service-minded hospitals recognize that a complaint is an opportunity to turn a dissatisfied customer into an ally if the organization provides a prompt apology and remedy for the problem.

High-performing hospitals recognize patient satisfaction as one of the most important indicators for consumer image and word-of-mouth marketing. Press-Ganey, the nation's largest satisfaction research firm, holds an annual client conference that attracts more than 1,000 hospitals to learn from best-in-class peers. The top-ranked Press-Ganey hospitals manage to achieve patient satisfaction above the 95th percentile level. High-scoring health institutions like Florida's Baptist Health Care and the Griffin Hospital in Derby, Connecticut, achieve superior ratings by persistent attention to service improvement and a sustained management commitment. Those institutions focus the attention of their senior management on addressing customer complaints, overcoming service barriers, and responding to employee suggestions for service improvement. Every week, at the top of the agenda, service is upper management's priority.

Consumer Input

Consultants advise clients to get close to consumers and improve skills in listening to them. How can this be achieved? Healthcare providers rely heavily on customer satisfaction measurement tools like patient surveys, focus groups, and telephone surveys. However, these methods may provide an incomplete picture of the consumers' real feelings and, worse yet, send the organization chasing off in the wrong direction to improve its services or products. The marketplace is littered with products—such as New Coke, the mammoth Ford Excursion, and online grocery delivery—that flopped despite extensive market research. Listening too closely to customers can lead to only incremental improvements in products or services rather than bold improvements that leave competitors scrambling to catch up. Instead, customers should be asked only for outcomes, that is, what they want a new product or service to do for them.

Direct Contracting

Direct contracting between purchasers and providers offers new market channels for best-of-class hospitals and physician groups. Employers who are increasingly frustrated with managed care and double-digit premium increases are now contemplating a move to direct contracting that would reduce or eliminate the role of the insurer as an intermediary. In Minnesota, the heartland of managed care, a large employer coalition has pushed HMOs into a secondary role, choosing to work directly with provider-organized networks of hospitals and doctors. Beginning in the late 1990s, the Buyers Health Care Action Group of Minneapolis–St. Paul shifted its strategy from buyers' clout to direct provider contracting after consolidation of local health plans left employers with few options and little price competition (Vinn 2000). More than a dozen provider networks volunteered to participate, and HMOs were only allowed to compete as network organizers with strict limitations on administrative expenses. The coalition carefully surveys patient perceptions about outcomes and makes the data available as employees and dependents select network options.

"Selling the Brand" Internally

In making marketing plans, hospitals may overlook one of the most important customer segments—their own employees. Marketing the brand *inside* the organization helps employees make a powerful emotional connection to the hospital's services and its patients. Colin Mitchell asks managers: "You tell customers what makes you great. Do your employees know?" (Mitchell 2002). Without strong internal support, employees may undermine the expectations set by the hospital's advertising and marketing. When employees know and believe in the brand, they are motivated to work harder and to tell the organization's story in positive terms.

Internal communication is essential so that employees know what service messages are being told to consumers. In worst-case scenarios, employees may be skeptical of the company's claims, or even disengaged and hostile toward management. Every hospital manager's worst service scenario is the situation in which an employee tells a patient, "I'm sorry I was slow to respond to your call light, but we're so short-staffed here we just can't properly take care of all our patients." Today's labor shortages and chronic staffing crises have created a difficult situation that requires a positive attitude and professional communications between caregivers and patients. Internal marketing must be consistently "on message" about putting patients first and backed up by visible examples of supervisors and managers doing the right thing for patients.

Great Leaders

Management theories of leadership have changed with every decade, and new theories abound. Some management experts believe that leadership is situational, where the successful leader is the right individual for the time. Others focus on the leader's role in communication of vision and values, both inside and outside the organization. Harvard's Michael Porter focuses on strategic wisdom, whereas Tom Peters argues on behalf of leaders who have a bias for action and are willing to "do it, try it, and fix it" (Porter 1999; Peters 1985). Jim Collins (2001) reports that it is definitely not the high-profile, charismatic executive who leaps from one industry to another, jump-starting lackluster businesses. In 9 of 11 companies he studied, firms that tried to revive themselves with a high-dollar boss from another successful firm were actually negatively affected. Those companies lost ground, and some lost substantial shareholder value.

STILL IN SEARCH OF EXCELLENCE (20 YEARS LATER)

American business in the 1980s was struck by lightning when top executives turned the pages of Peters and Waterman's (1982) *In Search of Excellence*. Many U.S. companies had been knocked for a loop by the arrival of foreign competitors, especially from Japan, that proved American goods—such as autos, cameras, computers, and copiers—to be overpriced and underperformers. Based at prestigious McKinsey & Co., a top business consulting firm, Peters and Waterman mined the databases on corporate performance. *In Search of Excellence* identified dozens of companies like Hewlett-Packard and Boeing that out-competed the market, and even the Japanese.

Peters and Waterman found many innovative organizations that excelled at product development, technical quality, customer service, and financial performance. These companies not only stood head-to-head with their Japanese counterparts, they had something to teach every organization:

> Excellent companies were, above all, brilliant on the basics. . . . These companies worked hard to keep things simple in a complex world. They persisted. They insisted on top quality. They fawned on their customers. They listened to their employees and treated them like

adults. They allowed their innovative product and service 'champions' long tethers. They allowed some chaos in return for quick action and regular experimentation. (Peters and Waterman 1982)

Finding the universal secrets that could set every business on the path to prosperity has been the "holy grail" of management science since the 1920s. Peters and Waterman were the latest in a long trail of management explorers like Frederick Taylor's scientific management in the 1920s, Elton Mayo's Hawthorne effect in the 1930s, Chester Bernard on leadership in the 1940s, Chris Argyris' Theory Z about human factors, and Daniel Bell predicting the transformational role of computers in business in the post-industrial 1970s.

American healthcare providers were largely shielded from foreign or even much more aggressive national competition until the past decade. The search-for-excellence message went largely unheeded in many hospitals and was unheard of by most physicians. Instead, healthcare providers were alarmed by the growing spread of managed care, an economically driven model of health insurance that placed tough new controls on hospital utilization and physician authority.

Twenty years later, the lessons of *In Search of Excellence* are once again relevant in the consumer-driven marketplace. Much of what Peters and Waterman said in the early 1980s is very instructive in today's competitive environment. The book was organized around the "seven S's"—structure, strategy, systems, skills, staff, style, and shared values. But the "happy atom" diagram of the seven S's was little more than a token gesture to their corporate consulting firm and to tradition. Deep down, Peters and Waterman had a message that many of their big clients would hate: small is beautiful, and smaller business units were often more nimble and closer to the customers than their top-down, central-planning bosses. Peters and Waterman focused on innovation as the key element that could be the make-or-break factor in unpredictable markets:

> We asserted that innovative companies not only are unusually good at producing commercially viable new widgets; *innovative companies are especially adroit at responding to change of any sort in their environments.* (Peters and Waterman 1982)

Both Peters and Waterman went on to write new books that extended the argument that small, customer-driven companies and business units could out-compete the largest multinational firms. Tom Peters' (1987) next book was *Thriving on Chaos*, and Bob Waterman (1994) authored *Adhocracy*. Forgetting the seven S's, Peters and Waterman distilled the lessons from best-run companies into eight messages.

1. *Bias for action.* Overcoming the bias of many companies toward "paralysis by analysis," the excellent companies had a bias for action. Peters and Waterman cited Digital Equipment Corporation as an example of a firm willing to pull the trigger on a new product or redesign.

2. *Close to the customer.* These successful companies learn from the customers they serve and provide unparalleled quality, service, and reliability. Companies include Frito-Lay, Maytag, and Tupperware, which succeeded in creating a reputation for excellence in product categories crowded with commodities.

3. *Autonomy and entrepreneurship.* Companies (like 3M) that foster innovation at every level nurture and honor their "champions."

4. *Productivity through people.* Treating the rank-and-file workers as the root source of quality and productivity is another hallmark of excellence. Southwest Airlines, IBM, and Texas Instruments are all examples of companies that place high value on their workforce.

5. *Hands on, value driven.* The "hands-on, value-driven" companies like Hewlett-Packard have a strong culture of managers who are closely involved in their products and services. David Packard and McDonald's founder Ray Kroc were famous for walking shop floors and visiting stores.

6. *Stick to the knitting.* Keeping a focus on the core business was a lesson that was contrary to the conglomerate model popular in the 1970s. Peters and Waterman took the opposite view, admonishing companies to "never buy a business you don't know how to run."

7. *Simple form, lean staff.* Unlike many companies of the 1980s that were managed by top-heavy matrix organizations, the companies Peters and Waterman chose had simple corporate structures with fewer than 100 people running billion-dollar businesses.

8. *Simultaneous loose-tight properties.* Although this principle seems almost an oxymoron, the excellent companies Peters and Waterman showcased had features of both centralization and decentralization. Companies like 3M push product development down to the shop

floor, resulting in home run products like Post-It notes, driven by a corporate emphasis on linking research and product development that kept the company innovative over decades.

Even 20 years later, hospitals and health organizations can still learn much from *In Search of Excellence*. The rise and fall of large integrated delivery systems in the 1990s was an instructive lesson in "stick to the knitting" and "simple form, lean staff."

Integrated delivery networks such as California's Catholic Healthcare West learned the hard way to divest noncore businesses like their physician network, downsize their ten-region overhead structure to four geographic divisions run by a very small top staff, and outsource their corporate business facility in Phoenix, Arizona, after spending hundreds of millions of dollars trying to centralize backroom functions. It is working. Catholic Healthcare West chief executive officer Lloyd Dean and the management team have the organization back in the black by renegotiating managed care contracts, achieving labor peace, and building new hospitals. It is an excellent company, and many more like it continue to exist among America's approximately 5,000 hospitals and 500 integrated delivery networks.

Peters and Waterman's admonishment to stay "close to the customer" is very timely in today's post–managed care consumer-choice market. When Peters and Waterman began looking for excellent companies in 1980, they initially focused on *Fortune* 500 firms that had high stock prices and excellent return-to-shareholder records. Ultimately, they found that financial success was only one measure of a truly excellent company and realized some of the best examples of innovation among lesser-known firms that were quicker to market with new ideas. Peters and Waterman ultimately discovered that building a culture of excellence was the secret of being an innovative and successful company.

Twenty years after the publication of *In Search of Excellence*, many American companies have adopted Japanese management approaches such as reliance on flexible work teams as the essential units of production and a continuous emphasis on quality to set a high standard. In healthcare, many innovative hospitals and integrated systems are using concepts like team nursing and continuous quality improvement.

In the health field, one can find many examples of excellent, value-driven health organizations: Boston's Brigham & Womens; Baptist Health Care in Pensacola, Florida; Memorial Herrman Healthcare

System in Houston, Texas; Sioux Valley Hospitals & Health System in Sioux Falls, South Dakota; Chicago's Northwestern Memorial Hospital; and even small, rural institutions like 49-bed Mid-Columbia Medical Center in The Dalles, Oregon. As hospitals, health systems, and medical groups prepare to compete on excellence, the message of *In Search of Excellence* is that the journey of becoming excellent is timeless and never complete.

STRATEGIC IMPLICATIONS FOR HOSPITALS, HEALTH SYSTEMS, AND PHYSICIAN ORGANIZATIONS

1. *Vision of excellence.* The most lasting visions are those that are shared by all stakeholders. Launch an organizationwide discussion focusing on the questions "How different will our future be from our past" and "How excellent could the organization become in tomorrow's environment?" Create a vision that could take 10 to 20 years to achieve, anticipating how the market will change and how competitors could respond. Ultimately, set the vision high enough so that no competitor is willing to go as far as your organization in striving for excellence.

2. *Benchmark with best of the best.* Pick a good company in the quest for excellence. Identify organizations that personify the values, higher goals, and beliefs that are similar to those of your institution. Become a "sister" organization. Interview their best people. Learn from their experience about what worked and where they fell short. Borrow their benchmarks and evaluation methods. If possible, engage in collaborative efforts, such as the Institute for Healthcare Improvement's rapid-cycle change initiatives for improving safety or customer satisfaction.

3. *Set high expectations, and meet them.* When the organization has reached its benchmark goals, it is time to move the bar higher. Do not be satisfied with good performance. Strive for greatness. Recognize the organization's champions who led successful initiatives and provided role models for the medical staff, nursing and allied health professionals, and rank-and-file employees. Set targets for high performance within the industry and for serving the community.

CONCLUSION

A culture of excellence is the core foundation of high performance. Management efforts to impose change are often frustrated by unspoken "foot dragging" and resistance from workers. "Culture eats strategy," advises Tom Rozek, chief executive officer of Miami Children's Hospital. Rozek's vision of excellence is paying off. Miami Children's was recently recognized as among the top 20 pediatric hospitals by *U.S. News & World Report*'s "Best Hospitals in America" (Rozek 2002). Culture cannot be changed overnight, or by a one-day training program. Becoming a learning organization is at the heart of culture building. Employees must understand what they need to change and develop skills specific to their roles in the organization.

Service consultant Gail Scott (2001b) advises managers to bring learning into the work environment, not the classroom, to make sure that lessons are grounded in the reality of job situations. The real key is shared values aligned with the goals and dreams of its key stakeholders: management, board, medical and nursing staff, and employees. A culture of excellence in which high performance is "good" is the platform for even higher levels of achievement—"great."

REFERENCES

Benko, L. S. 2002. "They've Got the Blues." *Modern Healthcare* 32 (38): 6, 12.

Berry, L. L. 1999. *Discovering the Soul of Service: The Nine Drivers of Sustainable Business Success.* New York: Free Press.

Carson, S. 2002. "RE-Shaping Healthcare." Conference notes. San Diego, California. September 29.

Comarow, A. 2002. "America's Best Hospitals: Honor Roll." *U.S. News & World Report* (July 22): 44–46.

Collins, J. 2001. *Good to Great: Why Some Companies Make the Leap and Others Don't.* New York: HarperBusiness.

Collins, J. C., and J. I. Porras. 1994. *Build To Last: Successful Habits of Visionary Companies.* New York: HarperBusiness.

D'Antonio, M. 2002a. "*U.S. News & World Report* Lists Yale–New Haven Among America's Best Hospitals." Press release. July 19.

———— 2002b. "Yale–New Haven Hospital Selected as a 2002 Most-Wired Award Winner by *Hospitals & Health Networks*." Press release. July 15.

Fox, S., and L. Rainie. 2002. "Vital Decisions: How Internet Users Decide What Information to Trust when They or Their Loved Ones Are Sick." Pew Internet & American Life Project, May 22, 1–43. Washington, DC: Pew Foundation.

George, J. 2002. "Blue Cross to Reward Hospitals for Quality." *Philadelphia Business Journal* (September 13–19): 1, 32.

Herzlinger, R. 1997. *Market Driven Health Care: Who Wins, Who Loses in the Transformation of America's Largest Service Industry*. Reading, MA: Perseus Books.

Hughes, T. 2002. "Forty-Five UNC Health Care Physicians Named 'Best Doctors' by *Business North Carolina*." Press release. July 2.

Mitchell, C. 2002. "Selling the Brand Inside." *Harvard Business Review* 80 (1): 99–105.

Peart, K. N. 2002. "Nine Yale Surgeons on *New York Magazine*'s List of Top 100 Minimally Invasive Surgeons." Press release. Feb. 1.

Peters, T. 1985. *A Passion for Excellence*. New York: Harper & Row.

———— 1987. *Thriving on Chaos*. New York: Harper Perennial.

Peters, T. J., and R. H. Waterman, Jr. 1982. *In Search of Excellence: Lessons From America's Best Run Companies*. New York: Harper & Row.

Porter, M. 1999. *Global Strategy*. Cambridge, MA: Harvard University Press.

Rozek, T. 2002. Personal communication, July.

Scott. G. 2001a. "The Voice of the Customer: Is Anyone Listening?" *Journal of Healthcare Management* 46 (4): 221–23.

———— 2001b. "Creating a Learning Environment: A 'Win-Win' Approach." *Journal of Healthcare Management* 46 (6): 361–64.

Solucient. 2003. *Solucient Top 100 Hospitals*. Evanston, IL: Solucient. 1–38.

———— 2001. *Cardiovascular Benchmarks for Success—2001: Top 100 Hospitals*. Evanston, IL: Solucient. 28.

Vinn, N. E. 2000. "The Emergence of Consumer-Driven Health Care." *Family Practice Management*. January. [Online article; retrieved 8/15/02.] www.aafp.org/fpm/20000100/46thee.html.

Waterman, R. H., Jr. 1994. *Adhocracy*. New York: W.W. Norton & Company, Ltd.

Working Mother. 2003. "The 100 Best Companies for Working Mothers List 2003." [Online information; retrieved 9/23/03.] www.workingwoman.com/100BestList.shtml.

Chapter 2

Positioning in a
Consumer-Driven Environment

According to just about every expert in the health field, the healthcare industry is witnessing the dawn of a new era— the age of the empowered healthcare consumer. Armed with unprecedented access to health-related information via the Internet, today's healthcare consumer is demanding more involvement in his or her own care as well as access to more choices as to how healthcare is organized, delivered and paid for.

—*Stephen Wilkins and Frederick Navarro (2001)*

AMERICAN DOCTORS AND hospitals are facing a new challenge—their patients. Consumerism is a powerful force that is motivating hospitals to monitor patient satisfaction and improve service levels. In the quiet sanctums of physician offices, Internet-empowered consumers are recreating the doctor-patient relationship. American healthcare is being forced to respond to retail medicine, where consumers are kings and queens of the market. Some healthcare executives may get "that old déjà vu feeling again," to paraphrase Yogi Berra, as they remember healthcare in the 1980s when health systems became branded, and hospitals brought in marketing managers from the private sector to direct multimillion-dollar advertising campaigns. In the twenty-first century, the consumer-choice market has returned.

FROM A WHOLESALE TO A RETAIL MARKET

Healthcare economics is undergoing a massive revolution. At the microeconomic level, with the declining power of managed care, patients do not have to struggle with gatekeepers to get referrals to specialists. In macroeconomic terms, the paradigm shift is from a wholesale market in the 1990s to a retail market in the new century. Healthcare is no longer a commodity, bought and sold at the cheapest price. Those hospitals most popular with consumers and large physician groups have been demanding and getting better reimbursement contracts from HMOs and managed care organizations.

Providers are confronting health plans on rates across the nation, publicly displaying their willingness to walk away from a bad contract. The providers' strategy of "push-back" is gaining considerable momentum. In a survey of 12 heavily managed care markets, providers were taking off the gloves over issues of reimbursement, loss of control, failure to pay claims promptly, and arbitrary claims denials (Draper et al. 2002). "Tiered-network plans" are the latest to incite plan-provider confrontation. Introduced last year, health plans such as California-based PacifiCare and Blue Shield on the West Coast and Tufts and Blue Cross/Blue Shield in Boston, grouped hospitals based on cost and then announced that enrollees would be charged a higher copayment to use the pricier facilities (Benko 2002). Providers were outraged, especially those hospitals that did not make the plans' "A-list." The North Bay Health System, a two-hospital integrated delivery network in the San Francisco Bay area, cancelled contracts with Blue Shield. In Boston, most of the high-cost hospitals were academic medical centers. So far, however, Massachusetts employers are not picking up the controversial tiered plans.

In a retail-type market, healthcare consumers are responding to service- and segment-specific advertising by hospitals and to direct-to-consumer marketing by pharmaceutical manufacturers. Healthcare executives are shifting gears to respond to the new marketplace. Filling beds is no longer the problem. Well-respected hospitals are full as the nation's health system is coping with a glut of demand. Growth is the challenge for America's $1.4 trillion health system between now and 2010. Demand for inpatient and ambulatory care services will rise steadily in the decade ahead, driven by demographics, consumerism, and technology. Emergency departments (EDs) are taxed to the limit to provide first-response care to the insured and uninsured. A 2001 survey by the American Hospital Association (AHA) found two in three hospitals reporting their EDs were at or over capacity. Urban hospital EDs were even more crowded, with 75 percent of EDs reaching their limits and being forced to route emergency patients to other hospitals (AHA 2001).

Hospitals like Chicago's Northwestern Memorial Hospital had the vision a decade ago to foresee the consumerism trend. Its vision became reality with a 500-bed total replacement facility that makes "patients first" (Briggs and Barnard 2000). The $580 million project responded to advice from over 1,000 consumers and providers in 125 user groups. The new facility integrates healing design and customer expectations based on an organizational culture of service. Sound planning and organizational vision have paid off: patient satisfaction scores, as measured by Press-Ganey, rose as much as 20 points in some categories after the new facility opened.

CONSUMER-DRIVEN HEALTHCARE PLANS

Benefits consultants tout the arrival of "consumer-driven" healthcare plans as the next wave of change in the health benefits and insurance industry (Gabel 2003). This is the "let's put consumers in charge of health care" scenario envisioned by Harvard Business School professor Regina Herzlinger. For consumers, Herzlinger states, choice equals power. In the field of investment and mutual funds, for example, consumer-driven information and control created enormous wealth for investors in a widespread financial revolution that now includes nearly 50 percent of all households invested in the stock market. She believes that 401(k)s are a good analogy to consumer-driven health plans (Herzlinger 2004). Both financial products and health plans are complex products, but the average consumers do surprisingly well in picking mutual funds.

Consumer-driven healthcare plans are the new product offerings that may replace HMOs and preferred provider organizations (PPOs) in the decade ahead. Innovative companies like Louisville, Kentucky–based Humana are in the forefront of the "personalized plan" movement, using powerful information systems that give the plans the ability to customize health offerings based on the preferences of individual customers. The new models offer enrollees more options, such as choosing their preferred providers and setting their own level of benefits and copayments. But consumers are also paying more for choice, with higher monthly premiums and bigger copayments for doctor visits and drugs that patients must pay for at the point of service. Consumer-based plans are still very new. In 2002, an estimated 1.5 million Americans were enrolled in one of the consumer-driven alternatives (Gabel 2003).

Gabel (2003) proposes the following three models of consumer-driven health plans.

1. *Personal spending account (PSA).* Designed like a "medical savings"–type plan offered to individuals by companies like Golden Rule, the personal spending account is financed by a monthly employer

contribution. The enrollee draws on the account when purchasing health services. If the amount is exhausted during the year, the employee usually faces a large deductible, which then changes the plan into a traditional health plan, usually a PPO. A typical PSA plan may have a $750 account with a deductible of $1,500. The incentive for the worker is the ability to roll over unused "savings" from one year to the next.

2. *Customized plan*. In this increasingly popular model, a single insurer offers an array of benefit designs and network sizes to an employer and its workers. Employers contribute a fixed amount, regardless of which plans their workers choose. In a typical customized plan, employees can select from three levels of benefits (low, medium, and high) and three network sizes (narrow, medium, and broad). The employee now has nine choices, each with a different premium. If the worker wants a choice that is more expensive than the employer's monthly contribution would cover, the employee "spends up" to pay the difference for his or her preferred option.

3. *Personalized plan*. A product of the information age, the "personalized plan" uses web-based tools that allow enrollees to form their personal network of physicians and hospitals while also selecting their own copayment levels. The choices of network, benefits, and copayments determine the worker's monthly premium. If this exceeds the employer's monthly contribution, the worker makes up the difference. The personalized plan is still quite new, and only a handful of insurers offer it.

CONSUMER BACKLASH SHIFTS ENROLLMENT FROM HMOS TO PPOS

Consumers have told the managed care industry what they thought about HMO gatekeepers and hassles whenever patients wanted to see specialists. They voted with their feet by leaving their HMOs; millions switched to consumer-friendly PPOs, even paying more for the option. The results have completely restructured the managed care industry. HMO enrollment peaked in 2000 at 81.4 enrollees and has since dropped by nearly 5 million, falling to 76.1 in 2002 (InterStudy Publications 2002). PPOs have been the beneficiary of consumer dissatisfaction with HMOs. PPO membership grew from 106 million in 1999 to 112 million by the end of 2001 (Aventis Pharmaceuticals 2002).

As a result, the differences between HMOs and PPOs are blurring. As health plan enrollment migrates toward less restrictive products, the market position of traditional HMOs like Kaiser and PacifiCare, which offer limited choice, becomes less attractive. In a recent survey of 50 managed care plans, virtually all were adding less restrictive products and restructuring existing products and policies (Draper et al. 2002). The trend to new, less restrictive products like "direct-access HMOs" demonstrates how managed care plans are responding to the market, especially in heavily penetrated HMO markets. In Phoenix, United Healthcare's direct-access product reportedly accounts for the majority of its membership. PacifiCare has begun offering a PPO in addition to its traditional HMO product, a major shift for a company whose past success has been based on its extensive delegation and risk sharing with network providers, mostly independent practice associations. Price differences are also narrowing. HMOs are shifting their market strategy from price leader to consumer friendly. Blue Cross of California is attempting to reposition its gatekeepers as "medical concierges."

THE NEW CONSUMERS: BOOMERS, BOBOS, HEALTH SEEKERS, AND THE WIRED RETIRED

Healthcare's new consumers—boomers, bobos, health seekers, and the wired retired—will be the thought leaders and market makers for healthcare in the decade ahead. They comprise healthcare's most influential consumers and create the demands driving up service volumes and capacity crises in operating and emergency rooms. They are Internet informed and empowered, changing the patient-physician relationship as they come to medical appointments armed with the latest medical literature.

These new consumer categories will dominate healthcare simply by their numbers. Although there is overlap across the groups, at least half of all Americans fall into one or more of these categories. And more than half of U.S. residents are women, who make an estimated 80 percent of their family's healthcare decisions (Wilkins and Navarro 2001). When healthcare organizations plan strategies for competing on excellence, they must consider rule number one: it's a consumer's world!

Boomers

The "age wave" Ken Dychtwald predicted over a decade ago is finally beginning to make an impact, as 50-somethings show the first signs of future chronic illness. Dychtwald (1989) predicted the following about the graying of the United States:

- Seniors will live longer than they expect—possibly much longer—as science brings the aging process under control.
- Older Americans will change their concept of family life (e.g., selling the family home and moving to an adult community).
- The physical environment will change to fit the pace, physiology, and style of a population predominantly in the middle and later years of life.
- Seniors may never retire or may retire several times.
- Growth of an older population will create an intergenerational tension—"age wars"—as consumers compete for limited resources.
- Middle-aged and older Americans will dominate politics, the economy, and society.

As the first baby boomers reach Medicare eligibility in the year 2010, this generation will take its place as healthcare's number one consumer and market maker. Today's baby boomers may be the biologically youngest generation of senior citizens the nation has ever known. They have a high level of health awareness, expanded by Internet access to health information from leading sources such as the Mayo Clinic and National Library of Medicine. And boomers plan to live to age 100, thanks to 40 minutes on their Stairmaster daily and consuming a diet rich in antioxidants and red wine. Boomers are also known as the "sandwich generation," caught between responsibilities for young children and aging parents. The role of women boomers is especially critical.

Bobos

Culture analyst David Brooks (2000), a senior editor for *Newsweek* and commentator on National Public Radio, calls them "'Bobos,' the elite spawn of the information age who combine the upwardly mobile middle class capitalism of the bourgeois with hippie attitudes of the bohemians." A new pecking order has emerged in American society, and it is led by these middle-aged, middle-class "new Bohemians." It is a new kind of meritocracy based on jobs and incomes, but not based on old money or "the rules." Bobos make money pursuing their vision. The leaders of this 30- to 50-something generation are more likely to be found in "new economy" professions like entertainment, journalism, technology, or research.

Bobos are the vanguard of a growing middle class that will be trend-setters and market makers in the next 10 to 20 years. The middle class is expanding, not shrinking, with much of the growth at the upper end. Within 10 years, ten million more American households will have incomes over $100,000; this is astonishing growth in two decades from 1982, when only 2 million were categorized as upper middle class. Education drives income, with a disproportionate share of the nation's wages and wealth now held by the college-educated elite, although only 20 percent of the U.S. population has a college degree. According to Brooks (2000), bobos are that elite.

You can spot bobos from the bottles of water sticking out of their backpacks or briefcases. They are very disciplined consumers, going online to get the lowest possible prices for cars or computers, but they will pay $4.75 for a loaf of specialty bread. They venerate nature. Affluent bobos are moving to upscale country locations like Camden, Maine; Asheville, North Carolina; and western Montana. Their health consciousness is high, their alcohol consumption is low, and they believe in mind-body integration and the spiritual aspects of health. Bobos are more likely to pass out business cards at a party than to pass out under the table.

Bobos will be thought leaders and market makers for healthcare in the decade ahead. Providers and the health system should respond with high technology, alternative medicine, Internet connectivity, healing environments, open communication, and a view of healthcare as a mission.

Health Seekers

In the information age, Internet-empowered health seekers are leading a revolution of informed consumers. According to Cyber Dialogue, a market research firm, an estimated 82 million, or 40 percent of all Americans, have Internet access (Wilkins and Navarro 2001). Some 50 percent of those with Internet access are designated health seekers by the Pew Foundation's Internet and American Life Project (Fox and Rainie 2000).

Health seekers use the Internet to find health information on a monthly basis—more frequently than for obtaining sports scores or other popular reasons for surfing the web. Demographically, health seekers are predominantly women between the ages of 30 and 50, typically college educated, with above-average income and health insurance. Harvard Business School professor Regina Herzlinger (1997), author of *Market-Driven Healthcare*, believes these health seekers will reform healthcare, just has they have changed retailing and financial services.

Hospitals are hearing the "Internet-empowered" message and joining their consumers on the World Wide Web. Three in five (58 percent) of U.S. hospitals have web sites, according to the latest annual survey by the American Hospital Association (2001). Joining the dot-com revolution is a little different in an industry dominated by not-for-profit facilities. About half of the hospital sites (47.7 percent) are "dot-orgs," while another 41.8 percent use "dot-com" to designate their site (other hospitals use the web address of their sponsoring organizations, such as "edu" for academic centers).

Web availability varies widely by region. Some 75 percent of hospitals in New England have web sites, while less than half (46.5 percent) of facilities in the eastern south-central region of the United States are Internet accessible to consumers. Large (over 300 beds) hospitals are three times as likely to offer a web site than the smallest facilities. Urban hospitals are 50 percent more likely to offer Internet access than their rural counterparts (AHA 2001).

Wired Retired

Healthcare's most active users—seniors—are flocking to the web. The rapid increase in seniors accessing the Internet has taken many market observers by surprise. The increase can be attributed to two trends: (1) younger retirees in the 60 to 70 age group who bring computer skills from their recent occupations and (2) older Americans who previously had no computer access but have become recipients of second-hand computers handed down from their children or grandchildren. Younger segments of the senior population use their computer skills to become familiar with early symptoms of chronic diseases, while older seniors find interest in new technology and how to optimize their health status.

Because marketing consultants believe that traditional marketing to mature consumers may miss as much as 40 percent of the senior population, pharmaceutical manufacturers are targeting health-conscious seniors with direct-to-consumer (DTC) marketing. Heavy spending on DTC marketing is increasingly shifting from lifestyle pharmaceuticals, like Claritan, to a variety of brand-name prescriptions for conditions such as heart disease, arthritis, and gastrointestinal conditions.

Older Americans can be differentiated according to their attitudes and behaviors with respect to healthcare products and services. Specialists at the J. Walter Thompson agency have identified eight segments of the mature market, including active achievers, true-blue believers, hearth and homemakers, fiscal conservatives, woeful worriers, intense individualists, liberal loners, and in-charge intellectuals (Snyder 2001).

CONSUMER CONCERN ABOUT QUALITY AND SAFETY

From a variety of sources, a national agenda for quality is gathering steam in the health field. The Institute of Medicine (IOM), in a ground-breaking report entitled *To Err is Human*, captured national headlines in 2000 with the announcement that 44,000 to 98,000 patients are killed each year by medical errors (Kohn, Corrigan, and Donaldson 2000). The IOM's blue-ribbon committee reviewed the medical literature on clinical performance and drew the conclusion that America's hospitals lack effective systems to identify medical errors or to systematically improve patient outcomes. The shocking report quickly drew the attention of provider organizations, major employers, and government agencies. If the report's assumptions are true, one in three inpatients are likely to experience a medical mishap during an average three-day hospital stay.

More recently, the Joint Commission on Accreditation of Healthcare Organizations has stepped up its pressure on hospitals to report sentinel events, such as deaths and medications errors, to counter concerns about massive underreporting of medical mistakes. America's voluntary health system still hopes to keep clinical performance measurement a non-governmental function. The National Quality Forum in Washington, DC, is working to establish a consensus on performance measures from a cross-section of health industry organizations, government agencies, and consumer groups.

The Leapfrog Group, an employer coalition of nearly 100 *Fortune* 500 companies, is creating a national scorecard on hospitals. Its goal is to improve patient safety and reduce medical errors. Leapfrog's standards include computerized physician order entry systems, physician intensivists to manage intensive care units, and volume standards for procedures such as open-heart surgery. On a targeted regional basis, Leapfrog is asking local hospitals to voluntarily report their level of compliance with Leapfrog standards, which will be publicized on their web site (www.leapfroggroup.org) and hot-linked to HealthGrades, Inc., a private company in Lakewood, Colorado, that offers comparative provider ratings. Not all hospitals are complying. The American Hospital Association has a mixed view of report cards and has been less than supportive of the Leapfrog Group's efforts to gather voluntary data on adherence to the group's volume and process criteria.

RATING HEALTHCARE PROVIDERS WITH REPORT CARDS

Will the release of data about clinical outcomes and patient satisfaction make hospitals more accountable to the public and to purchasers? None of us really knows the best hospital for a heart bypass or a liver transplant. The lack of information can make choosing a quality hospital network a crapshoot (Bryant 2000a). A major experiment in consumer-led health-care is about to begin that will reveal hospital data and even physician performance. America's hospitals, physicians, and health insurance companies will soon find themselves in the harsh spotlight of comparative public information. Government agencies and employers are creating dozens of report card coalitions to inform consumers and companies about which providers and health plans have the best health outcomes and patient satisfaction ratings.

Within the next two to five years, the federal government could adopt a report card for Medicare-participating hospitals. Tom Scully, the head of the Centers for Medicare and Medicaid Services (CMS) has suggested that Medicare may pay more for quality to top-rated hospitals and doctors at some time in the future. CMS has issued a request for information to healthcare market research organizations that measure patient satisfaction. CMS hopes to identify potential questions for a federal survey.

Another federal bureau, the Agency for Healthcare Research and Quality, has developed a prototype report card in response to a request from Congress. A number of state health and insurance agencies are already compiling report cards on providers and HMOs. The report card concept is becoming an international trend as well. In Canada, the government of Ontario and the Ontario Hospital Association are collaborating on a series of reports profiling acute care performance based on research by the hospital association (Government of Ontario 2001).

Several companies are vying for the role as the "J.D. Powers" of the health industry, whose rankings are a coveted symbol of customer satisfaction. Solucient, a healthcare market research firm in Evanston, Illinois, awards annual recognition to the top 100 hospitals and also recognizes the top 100 in specialty medicine such as cardiac care and emergency services. HealthGrades operates a web site (www.healthgrades.com) that rates hospital specialty services on a five-star basis, based on Medicare data. Consumer groups such as the California Healthcare Foundation are joining the report card movement, compiling and publishing patient satisfaction ratings on a hospital-specific basis. New York–based Health Care Choices is a nonprofit organization that educates consumers about the health system and advises individuals on finding and choosing a health plan or HMO (Rosenfeld 2002). Funded in part by the United Way, the consumer group also provides information about hospitals and doctors, including surgical volume data and physician profiles.

PAYING FOR PERFORMANCE

Coalitions of purchasers have backed the development of measurement systems such as the Health Plan Employer Data and Information Set (HEDIS) as a way to directly compare competing providers and, in a few cases, pay higher rates for above-benchmark performance. Payers have also engaged in limited instances of exclusive contracting to centers of excellence as well as to medical groups based on a combination of cost and qualitative performance.

In San Francisco, the Pacific Business Group on Health (PBGH) has issued reports grading California HMOs as well as large physician groups. PBGH has experimented with paying physician groups a bonus for higher performance on HEDIS benchmarks and patient survey data or penalizing a low-performing group with reduced payments. But few groups have been willing to play the ratings game.

At the national level, the Leapfrog Group is rolling out a data-collection effort to measure compliance with Leapfrog standards. Leapfrog members in New York, including GE and AT&T, are collaborating with Empire Blue Cross Blue Shield to offer a bonus to hospitals that achieve compliance with some or all Leapfrog measures. A $2 million bonus pool will be distributed by Empire as a percentage increase in payments over the course of three years (Freudenheim 2001).

BEST OF THE BEST: BECOMING A TOP 100, BEST HOSPITAL IN AMERICA, OR FIVE STAR

An elite cadre of hospitals is becoming recognized as the best places in America for all-around quality and specialized inpatient treatments. At the local level, top-ranked hospitals are using their ratings to burnish reputations as regional, national, and—for the very best—international centers of excellence.

Solucient 100 Top Hospitals

Since 1993, Solucient (formerly HCIA/Sachs) has recognized 100 hospitals for their excellence in efficient management and quality outcomes (Solucient 2000). Solucient grades hospitals on a peer-to-peer basis, evaluating against eight performance measures. The 100 top hospitals demonstrate high standards of efficiency and effectiveness. Despite more acute and complex patients, Solucient's 100 top hospitals have better outcomes, operate with fewer staff per patient, and achieve higher levels of profitability.

Employers are impressed with Solucient's analysis, which demonstrates that business practices such as benchmarking and Six Sigma are paying off in the 100 top hospitals (Service 2000). Solucient's 2002 ratings were delayed when CMS extended the deadline for 2000 Medicare cost reports, but Solucient returned to annual rankings in 2003 for the overall top 100 and selectively released top 100 ratings for other specialty services.

U.S. News & World Report's "Best Hospitals in America"

For more than a decade, *U.S. News & World Report* has been publishing its annual listing of the "Best Hospitals in America." The nation's best-known academic medical centers—Johns Hopkins, the Mayo Clinic, The Cleveland Clinic, Massachusetts General, and UCLA Medical Center—have consistently placed in the top five based on the number of their medical programs considered the best in the nation. The report recognizes the top-rated clinical programs in 18 categories, including heart, cancer, orthopedics, obstetrics, pediatrics, urology, psychiatry, and other specialties.

In most categories, up to 50 hospitals are ranked according to a composite score that reflects physician preferences and Medicare outcomes data. There is one qualification for the best hospital designation. The institution must be a member of the Council of Teaching Hospitals, a pool of nearly 500 academic medical centers and teaching hospitals, of which 205 are cited for excellence in at least one clinical program in the 2002 rankings (*U.S. News & World Report* 2002).

HealthGrades Five-Star Ratings

The five-star ratings from HealthGrades have become prized symbols of quality care in hundreds of hospitals across the United States. The company operates a national web site, www.healthgrades.com, designed to help consumers identify and select hospitals with the best track records in a variety of clinical services and procedures, including the categories of cardiology, orthopedics, neurosciences, pulmonary/respiratory, obstetrics, and vascular surgery. Based on three years of MedPar (Medicare) data and the company's proprietary rating system, HealthGrades assigns a three-level ranking to each clinical service. Five-star (better than expected), three-star (as expected), and one-star (worse than expected) rankings give prospective patients an easily understood comparison of hospitals in a region or state.

Some 15 percent of hospital services rated by HealthGrades are awarded five stars, and 70 percent receive three stars. HealthGrades is also collaborating with the Leapfrog Group and posting Leapfrog's ratings for every hospital that has completed a Leapfrog survey on the HealthGrades web site. Additional ratings are offered for nursing homes, home health agencies, hospices, and fertility clinics. A HealthGrades directory of 620,000 physicians is searchable by specialty and location, but it provides no physician rankings. HealthGrades offers top-rated hospitals a package of quality assessment and improvement tools and a regional exclusive marketing license to the five-star ranking in their service area (Health-Grades 2002).

STATE REPORT CARDS PUT HOSPITALS IN THE SPOTLIGHT

In state capitals across the nation, legislators are not waiting for Washington to come up with a national report card on hospitals or health plans. An increasing body of evidence shows that best practices produce higher quality at lower cost (Lippman 2002). But how and where do consumers get the best? Nearly ten states, including California, Georgia, Maryland, New York, Pennsylvania, Rhode Island, Texas, and Wisconsin have created report cards that rate health providers and HMOs and are publishing the scorecards on the Internet and through the media. The programs in four of these states are described below.

California

California consumers have a variety of report cards to help make decisions about hospitals and doctors. The Office of Statewide Health Planning and Development publishes hospital-specific statistics on acute myocardial infarction (mortality), intensive care units (mortality), hip fracture (mortality), maternal outcomes following delivery (readmissions), and pneumonia (mortality). The state also issues a periodic report with risk-adjusted data on coronary arterial bypass graft procedures in 118 California hospitals offering heart surgery (Office of Statewide Health Planning and Development 2002).

The most controversial report was backed by the California HealthCare Foundation, which funded the PEP-C study (Patients' Evaluation of Performance in California), a statewide patient satisfaction research project that asked 21,000 patients to rate their care (California HealthCare Foundation 2002). Consumer guides are available for northern and southern California and published in English, Spanish, and Chinese. Hospital participation was voluntary, and only 113 hospitals were willing to be rated, about 30 percent of the state's acute care facilities. Hospitals were graded in a three-tier scheme: above average, average, and below average.

Maryland

The Maryland Health Care Commission has issued a consumers' guide to Maryland's 52 hospitals (Maryland Health Care Commission 2002). The report provides a limited set of quality indicators and also reports on hospitals' performance in treating medical conditions. After several years of debate, the Maryland General Assembly authorized the guide in 1999, despite hospital arguments that some facilities could be penalized by poor report card grades because they treat older, sicker patients (Werner 1999).

Texas

In response to provider complaints and consumer concerns about managed care, the state of Texas has issued a report card on 34 large HMOs, which represent about 90 percent of commercial enrollment in the state. The state Office of Public Insurance Counsel is responsible for the report, "Comparing Texas HMOs 1998, Ratings by Consumers" (Turner 1998). Consumers were asked to rate satisfaction with their health plans in specific areas of quality of care and physician services, for both primary care and physician specialists. Most plans tallied average scores, but some HMOs received a below-average rating from their enrollees.

Wisconsin

A statewide report on HMOs has noted improved service ratings since the report was inaugurated in 1995 (Sneider 1997). Two dozen Wisconsin managed care plans were reviewed in the report "It's Your Choice," compiled by the administrator of insurance services for the Wisconsin Department of Employee Trust Funds. The report is issued to 210,000 state and public employees, dependents, and retirees who receive their health benefits through the trust fund. Media publicity has made the guide a public service and has laid the groundwork for a partnership between the state and The Alliance, a Madison-based employer coalition.

PUSHING BACK OR COOPERATING, PROVIDERS WILL HAVE CONSUMER ACCOUNTABILITY

Hospitals and doctors are being dragged, sometimes kicking and screaming, into the spotlight of public disclosure. The demand for public accountability is coming from major employers, elected officials, and consumer groups.

The momentum could even lead to federal regulations over error reporting. Providers continue to resist some disclosure demands, such as the Leapfrog Group, for conformance to volume standards that providers believe are arbitrary or do not necessarily produce quality care. Providers also criticize quality rating systems that may not account for sicker patients, differences in population demographics, and inefficiencies of data-reporting programs.

Provider foot-dragging about disclosure is more than anxiety about public embarrassment. Concerns about malpractice are very close to the surface. Dr. Donald Patten of Crisp Regional Hospital in Cordele, Georgia, comments about Georgia's new report card: "If you report an error for the sake of educational efforts, you open yourself up to attack. I wish it were different, but I will say that doctors are committed to improving these hospitals" (Bryant 2000b).

Healthcare providers fear that public disclosure of medical mishaps will open the door to costly malpractice suits, pushing thousands of physicians out of practice and driving up hospital costs with million-dollar legal battles. Small providers, such as rural hospitals or home health agencies, could be bankrupted by a single costly malpractice incident. To quell provider concerns, experts have suggested a no-fault reporting system such as the one used by the airlines. Paul Shaner, executive director of the Medical Association of Georgia, suggests there is a strong rationale for adopting the air industry's approach: "The airline industry doesn't report every near-miss or every problem they have. They try to get the most reporting they can get to improve quality" (Bryant 2000b).

STRATEGIC IMPLICATIONS FOR HOSPITALS, PHYSICIANS, AND HEALTH PLANS

1. *Play the ratings game.* Assume that report cards will profile every hospital in the nation over 50 beds. If rankings and ratings are the name of the game, learn what criteria are used by the rating systems in your market. Assess your position in the ratings game versus

competitors on a regional or statewide basis. Inform the board, management team, medical and nursing staff, and rank-and-file employees where you stand, and set goals for achieving top rankings.

2. *Physician leadership*. Enhancing clinical performance and patient satisfaction are the keys to quality improvement. Strong physician leadership is crucial to improving outcomes and satisfaction. Appoint or recruit a physician executive to manage quality improvement. This is a full-time job in larger healthcare institutions and integrated systems. Inform the medical staff and clinical departments of where your organization stands in the ratings. Doctors respond to data and evidence-based medicine. Benchmark your performance against top 100 or five-star facilities. Identify performance gaps. Create an internal dialog about the ratings criteria most important to your stakeholders and set internal objectives.

3. *Health plan–provider relations*. Quality improvement is an opportunity for collaboration between health plans and providers and a chance to rebuild relationships that were damaged in the managed care wars of the 1990s. Both plans and providers need to come together around the customer. Quality is an internal process, but it can be stimulated by external factors like health plan report cards. HMOs and insurers can employ ratings as a challenge to motivate performance improvement. Create financial incentives and bonus pools to reward positive gains. For hospitals whose performance is above benchmark standards, recognize those institutions as centers of excellence. Health plans should make investments that will assist providers in their networks to improve clinical outcomes and patient satisfaction (e.g., information systems, patient satisfaction surveys, and service-line data).

CONCLUSION

Focusing on the consumer is a complete shift from the 1990s, when bargaining with managed care plans was the critical success factor. Finance must now make room for marketing in the executive suite. The key to success in the decade ahead is satisfying the growing healthcare demands of millions of Internet-empowered baby boomers and seniors. Patients want it all: access to the latest technology, prompt treatment, courteous service—and, of course, free valet parking.

Some healthcare executives may still not be sold on the retail market scenario. Is this consumer-driven market a passing phase or a long-term phenomenon that will force every provider to fundamentally realign its strategies to compete on quality? Michael Stocker, M.D., the chief executive officer of Empire Blue Cross Blue Shield in New York, remains skeptical: "Hospitals have been led down many paths in the past that have turned out to be dead-ends. . . . It's hard to make the business case for quality, but we're trying. If a hospital is an early adopter, it should have an advantage" (Freudenheim 2001). In the face of consumerism, some provider organizations will choose not to compete on quality and will overlook the most critical success factor—focusing on the patient.

NOTE

Parts of the "The New Consumers: Boomers, Bobos, Health Seekers, and the Wired Retired" section in this chapter are adapted from Russ Coile's *Health Trends*, March 2002, 14 (5): 1–9.

REFERENCES

American Hospital Association (AHA). 2001. *Hospital Statistics 2000–2001.* Chicago: Health Forum.

Aventis Pharmaceuticals. 2002. "HMO-PPO/Medicare-Medicaid Digest." *Managed Care Digest Series.* Bridgewater, NJ: Aventis 66–67.

Benko, L. 2002. "Controversial Plans Are Here to Stay, Insurers Say." *Modern Healthcare* 32 (22): 17.

Briggs, P. J., and C. Barnard. 2000. "The New Northwestern Memorial Hospital: Planned, Constructed and Operated Through the Patients First Philosophy." *Journal on Quality Improvement* 26 (5): 287–98.

Brooks, D. 2000. *Bobos in Paradise: The New Upper Class and How They Got There.* New York: Simon & Schuster.

Bryant, J. 2000a. "Employers Press for Access to Data." *Atlanta Business Journal* October 9. [Online article; retrieved 10/21/02.] http://www.atlanta.bizjournals.com/stories/2000/10/09/story2.html.

Bryant, J. 2000b. "Georgia Hospitals Under Microscope." *Atlanta Business Journal* October 9. [Online article; retrieved 10/21/02.] http://www.atlanta.bizjournals.com/atlanta/stories/2000/10/9/story1.html.

California HealthCare Foundation. 2002. "PEP-C Report: What Patients Think of California Hospitals." [Online article; retrieved 10/21/02.] http://www.chcf.org/documents/quality/PEPCTechReport.pdf.

Draper, D. A., R. E. Hurley, C. S. Lesser, and B. C. Strunk. 2002. "The Changing Face of Managed Care." *Health Affairs* 21 (1): 11–23.

Dychtwald, K. 1989. *Age Wave: The Challenges and Opportunities of an Aging America.* Los Angeles: J. P. Tarcher.

Fox, S., and L. Rainie. 2000. "The Online Health Care Revolution: How the Web Helps Americans Take Better Care of Themselves." Pew Internet & American Life Project. Washington, DC: Pew Foundation Nov. 26. 1–23.

Freudenheim, M. 2001. "Companies Start Fund to Reward Hospitals for Better Care." *New York Times* October 18, C3.

Gabel, J. 2003. "The Next Wave in Payment Looms." *Modern Healthcare* 33 (1): 23.

Government of Ontario. 2001. *Hospital Report Cards*. Ontario, Canada: Ministry of Health and Long-Term Care. July 12.

HealthGrades. 2002. "10-K Filing: HealthGrades, Inc." Securities and Exchange Commission, Quarterly filing, April 1, 1–95. Lakewood, CO: HealthGrades, Inc.

Herzlinger, R. 1997. *Market-Driven Healthcare*. Cambridge, MA: Harvard Business School Press.

————. 2004. *Consumer-Driven Healthcare*. San Francisco: Jossey-Bass.

InterStudy Publications. 2002. *Competitive Edge: HMO Industry Report 12.2* Minneapolis, MN: InterStudy Publications, p. ix.

Kohn, L., J. Corrigan, and M. Donaldson. 2000. *To Err Is Human: Building a Safer Health System*. Washington, DC: National Academy Press, Institute of Medicine.

Lippman, H. 2002. "Front and Center: Defining Excellence in Specialized Care." *Business & Health* (June 3) 1–7. [Online article; retrieved 10/22/02.] http://www.businessandhealth.com.

Maryland Health Care Commission. 2002. "Maryland Hospital Performance Guide," August 9. [Online press release; retrieved 10/22/02.] http://www.mhcc.state.md.us.

Office of Statewide Health Planning and Development. 2002. "California Health Outcomes Project." State of California, Department of Health, February 8. [Online article; retrieved 10/21/02.] http://www.oshpd.gov.ca.us.

Rosenfeld, S. 2002. "Health Care Choices." [Online article; retrieved 8/17/02.] http://www.info@healthcarechoices.org.

Service, R. 2000. "Myth and Management in American Hospitals: You Can't Just Spend Your Way to Quality." *Business & Health* 19 (4): 28–32.

Sneider, J. 1997. "HMO Performance Improves with State Monitoring System." *Business Journal of Milwaukee*. [Online article; retrieved 10/21/02.] http://www.milwaukee.bizjournals.com/milwaukee/stories/1997/10/20/story5.html.

Snyder, R. 2001. "Market Segmentation: Successfully Targeting the Senior Population." *COR Healthcare Market Strategist* 2 (10): 14–17.

Solucient. 2000. "100 Top Hospitals: Benchmarks for Success." Evanston, IL: Solucient. 1–38.

Turner, M. 1998. "HMOs Receive Report Card from Consumers." *San Antonio Business Journal*. [Online article; retrieved 10/19/02.] http://www.sanantonio.bizjournals.com/sanantonio/stories/1998/10/26/story7.html.

U.S. News & World Report. 2002. "Best Hospitals: Honor Roll." [Online article; retrieved 10/22/02.] http:// www.usnews.com.

Werner, B. 1999. "Legislature to Explore Hospital Grading." *Baltimore Business Journal.* [Online article; retrieved 10/18/02.] www.baltimore.bizjournals.com/baltimore/ stories/1999/01/18/story.html.

Wilkins, S. T., and F. H. Navarro. 2001. "Has the Web Really Empowered Health Care Consumers?" *Marketing Health Services* (Fall): 1–5.

Chapter 3

Market Strategies for Revenue Growth

Healthcare providers have struggled through an extremely difficult period where survival was the main goal; those that have emerged, battered and bruised but somewhat intact, need to balance continued cost vigilance with a growth orientation before the next shock hits.

—Alan M. Zuckerman and Tracy K. Johnson (2001)

"GROW OR DIE" is a mantra commonly heard in business. But growth at any cost is a prescription for failure, as Enron and WorldCom—and some of the high-flying healthcare integrated delivery systems formed in the 1990s—can attest. Nonetheless, growth is essential to fuel the drive for excellence and, as described in the preface and first chapter of this book, is an essential characteristic of high-performing companies. Growth needs to occur in healthcare organizations, but in a much more thoughtful and purposeful way than has typically been the case in the past.

The 1990s have been referred to as the most turbulent, chaotic, and volatile years ever experienced by the healthcare industry. The late 1990s in particular saw most healthcare organizations experience declining and even plummeting financial performance. Excess supply, price and reimbursement pressures, the accumulated effects of managed care, and the lingering effects of the Balanced Budget Act of 1997 have forced many healthcare organizations into their second or third wave of cost repositioning.

Significant efforts are also under way to maximize reimbursement, improve coding accuracy, implement more thorough charge-capture mechanisms, and review managed care contracts and payer compliance. But as organizations pursue what seem to be endless rounds of financial performance improvement activities, a few aggressive and innovative providers are breaking out of the cost-cutting cycle and pursuing new sources of revenue.

Why has revenue growth been overlooked or relegated to a minor role? Few revenue-growth opportunities can demonstrate the dramatic and rapid improvements in financial performance that cost-repositioning strategies can. But revenue growth can provide significant and long-term benefits, in financial terms and improved patient care and access, and should be considered a powerful tool for coping with ongoing financial pressures.

Revenue growth plays off of and feeds increasing excellence and the ability of an organization to compete by being better. Organizations that excel should capture larger volumes by increasing market areas and growing share. These increased patient volumes and incremental revenues should generate greater margins that provide the funding stream for future improvement. In contrast, it is highly unlikely that any organization could shrink its way to distinction and success.

FIVE STRATEGIES FOR REVENUE GROWTH

There are five key revenue-growth strategies, all of which are being employed to varying degrees by healthcare organizations, but rarely in a systematic or purposeful manner.

1. *Increase market share.* Expand the breadth and depth of existing services, such as adding new capabilities.
2. *Expand the service area.* Develop programs with broader market draw or establish new delivery sites on the periphery of the existing service area.
3. *Fill gaps in the continuum of services.* Partner with others or develop new services not currently provided by the organization.
4. *Develop niche services.* Seek opportunities to provide profitable niche programs.
5. *Use market segmentation.* Organize services by market segment or disease (e.g., women's health center, spine center, etc.).

Increase Market Share

The most basic of the five revenue-growth strategies is increasing market share. Years of shrinking acute care demand and fierce competition for fewer patients led to an emphasis on system consolidation and nonacute services development in the 1990s. But signs are now emerging that the time is right to consider strengthening core services and increase organizations' share of the acute services market. Acute care services persist as a significant line of services for most hospitals and systems. After several years of flat or declining utilization, admission rates and emergency visit rates are increasing (AHA 2001), with further increases anticipated as the population grows and ages.

A variety of approaches exist for increasing market share, such as increasing patient satisfaction, expanding service lines, and marketing centers of excellence. However, three specific approaches have demonstrated proven returns in many markets:

1. Physician recruitment and medical staff development
2. Improved and enhanced emergency services and capabilities
3. Subspecialty service development

In each case, the focus is on increasing the range and scope of services available, thus emphasizing the excellence of services offered.

Physician Recruitment and Medical Staff Development

The failure of physician practice management companies and the drastic operating losses experienced by hospitals and systems that owned physician practices have left many hospitals and physicians feeling disillusioned about integrated service delivery. As alliances shift and realign in the coming years, opportunities may emerge for hospitals and systems to craft new relationships with primary care physicians and specialists to broaden referral bases and service mixes.

Medical staff manpower studies can help determine an organization's need for physicians by specialty based on service area population, the health needs of the community, and the program-specific targeted market shares that reflect key strategic goals. The medical staff needs analysis performed at one community hospital in 2001 (illustrated in Figure 3.1) revealed several opportunities. The analysis showed that the hospital's primary care physicians were not well developed in the primary and secondary services areas. Existing obstetrics/gynecology groups would not be able to achieve the system's market share targets, and medical staff deficits were projected in medical cardiology, general surgery, orthopedics, and neurology and neurosurgery.

By ensuring that medical staffs have sufficient breadth and depth, hospitals and systems can strengthen hospital admission rates and referrals to ancillary services. A full-time, productive, primary care physician with

Figure 3.1   Medical Staff Needs Analysis for a Community Hospital

Specialty	Projected Physician FTE Need	Projected Phsyician FTE Supply	FTE Surplus/ (Deficit)
Adult Primary Care			
Primary service area	65	46	(19)
Secondary service area A	9	2	(7)
Secondary service area B	13	1	(12)
Secondary service area C	11	0	(11)
Obstetrics/Gynecology	25	13	(12)
Medical Specialties			
Cardiology	9.0	5.5	(3.5)
Gastroenterology	5.4	6.9	1.5
Neurology	5.4	3.0	(2.4)
Pulmonary	3.4	5.2	1.8
Surgical Specialties			
General surgery	9.9	7.4	(2.5)
Neurosurgery	2.4	0.9	(1.5)
Orthopedics	12.5	7.8	(4.7)
Plastic surgery	3.2	4.4	1.2

Note: FTE = full-time equivalent.
Source: Health Strategies & Solutions, Inc. 2003. Used with permission.

a base of 2,000 patients may generate up to 200 direct and indirect admissions annually. Admissions by specialists vary significantly, but the point to be driven home is that even slight medical staff shortages can have a dramatic impact on hospital revenues.

Improved and Enhanced Emergency Services

As the main gateway into a hospital, an emergency department (ED) can generate up to 60 percent or more of all admissions (Delaware Valley Healthcare Council 1999; Broward Regional Health Planning Council 2000). The emergency department is often the community's first contact with the hospital, placing the ED in the key role of establishing the patient's relationship to an acute care provider.

Managed care initiatives have diverted some nonurgent visits to physician offices or express care centers, but emergency visits have risen in recent years, increasing to 364 visits per 1,000 population in 1999 after bottoming out at 347 visits per 1,000 population in 1997 (AHA 2001). Consumer backlash over denied coverage and creation of criteria for patients seeking ED care are likely to thwart any further efforts by managed care companies to reduce ED utilization.

Urgent and emergent visits form the direct link between the magnitude of ED visits and hospital admissions. Generally, the more ED visits a provider handles, the great the number of resulting admissions. To the extent that ED expansion would improve access to healthcare, increase patient satisfaction, and generate positive revenue streams, hospitals and systems should ensure efficient departmental and system operations in the ED and expand service capabilities to satisfy unmet needs.

Subspecialty Service Development

Improving subspecialty services provides a number of benefits for healthcare organizations. Providing care previously unavailable locally enables hospitals and systems to further their mission by meeting community needs while also reducing outmigration for specialty care and treatment. Two key factors have made opportunities to enhance subspecialty care services even more attractive. First, technology diffusion has made it possible to provide some subspecialty services in community hospitals and freestanding centers rather than exclusively at major tertiary medical centers. Second, horizontal integration and the formation of regional multihospital systems have provided opportunities for providers to share the costs and resources needed to develop new capabilities.

Now is the time for healthcare organizations to move from the mindset of minimizing resource expenditures for a defined group of covered lives to reassessing their marketplaces and aggressively seeking out opportunities to capitalize on the longstanding core business of hospitals and systems—strong, efficient, and effective acute care services.

Expand the Service Area

Extending services areas, usually into adjacent markets, has also been a frequently employed strategy among healthcare organizations. Increasing the geographic reach of hospitals and systems increases the number of people accessing services and boosts revenues.

The following four principal approaches can expand an organization's service area:

1. Affiliating with or acquiring other providers near the boundary or outside of the service area
2. Developing highly specialized services that draw patients from a greater geographic area
3. Enhancing community outreach programs to reach new patient populations
4. Establishing new delivery sites near the boundary or outside the service area

Affiliating with or Acquiring Other Providers

Affiliating with or acquiring other providers may enable healthcare organizations to enter new markets, expand their service areas, and possibly expand the range of services offered to achieve growth and increase revenues. A wide range of affiliation opportunities exists, from strategic alliances to joint ventures to mergers and acquisitions, with each varying in the degree of operational and organizational integration.

Unlike the other approaches to expanding the service area discussed in this chapter, affiliation or acquisition is a "buy" versus "make" strategy. The buy approach is often employed when there is a sense of urgency or a window of opportunity, a shortage of internal resources to manage the expansion, and strong complementarity among the organizations seeking to work together, whether these organizations are hospitals, systems, or physician practices.

Mercy Health System is an excellent example of employing the buy approach to expand its service area. In the early 1990s, Mercy Health System, which included three community hospitals located in the metropolitan Philadelphia, Pennsylvania, market where there was little or no population growth, purchased a fourth hospital in a fast-growing suburban community. The system then signed a contract to manage a two-hospital system in North Philadelphia. These initiatives, along with the system's managed care plan, Mercy Health Plan, have now made Mercy Health System the largest multistate Medicaid managed care organization in the country.

Developing Highly Specialized Services

Developing tertiary or quaternary services extends the service area and potentially increases revenue by providing a more convenient and accessible alternative. A "halo" effect may also be created, with the new service attracting more patients for all services and generating increased volumes of ancillary tests and procedures.

To fast-track development of specialized services and capitalize on brand-name recognition, providers can partner with market leaders (e.g., a community hospital affiliating with a children's hospital to provide pediatric subspecialty services). Before launching highly specialized services, thorough feasibility studies should be performed, since some programs need rather large service area populations to be cost effective.

Enhancing Community Outreach Programs

The strategy of enhancing community outreach programs includes a variety of initiatives such as marketing existing services to populations residing outside the existing service area and developing programs to reach new populations by using collaborative models. For example, Saint Raphael Health System in New Haven, Connecticut, reached beyond its immediate neighborhood to operate school-based clinics, clinics for seniors, a mobile obstetric unit, a home care network, and a parish nurse program in more than 20 churches.

Community outreach initiatives may also gather valuable information about the health needs of new and growing populations, enabling providers to expand their service area while positively affecting the health status of the community.

Establishing New Delivery Sites

The final method for expanding a hospital's geographic reach is to establish delivery sites near the boundary or beyond the existing service area. In fast-growing markets, new acute care facilities are needed. A more common occurrence is developing an ambulatory care site with services tailored to the surrounding community.

A number of benefits can emerge from these new sites, including increased access to services, greater community awareness of a provider organization, opportunities to partner with physicians or physician groups that could increase inpatient referrals and outpatient activity, potential new revenue streams, and the opportunity to protect or enhance the organization's inpatient market share in communities surrounding the new site.

Fill Gaps in the Continuum

Rather than go head-to-head against other hospitals and systems, many healthcare organizations have opted to fill gaps in service availability. For many years, and as late as the 1980s in some regions, gaps could be easily discovered and filled with little or no impact on other providers in the market. But as gaps have disappeared, this strategy has become difficult to pursue. Instances still occur where real community needs are not being met, and healthcare organizations, alone or in partnership with others, can provide these services efficiently and effectively.

Medicare reimbursement changes, past failures of vertical integration, and a retreat from full capitation have led some providers to question the value of providing or having access to all components of the continuum; however, planning within the continuum-of-care framework is still a valuable approach. Reviewing services currently provided along the continuum, particularly within existing product lines, can reveal feasible opportunities for some healthcare organizations to pursue.

Two types of continua are useful to review: the patient care continuum and the clinical-service-line continuum. These frameworks may overlap, but their unique aspects enable healthcare organizations to most easily identify service gaps.

Patient Care Continuum

Figure 3.2 illustrates the continuum of care for five key patient settings: pre-entry, acute, subacute, outpatient, and home care. A sample of services for each setting is also included. When an organization's existing services are arrayed against this type of framework, gaps in the continuum can be identified. This analysis can be augmented by evaluating patient referral and discharge information to determine how frequently patients are referred to other settings or if bottlenecks occur when transitioning patients to different levels of care due to a shortage of providers, capacity, or processes to manage the transition.

One stage of the patient care continuum often overlooked is pre-entry or pre-provider services that link patients to the healthcare system and provide entry to the rest of the continuum. Services such as adequate emergency medical services systems, senior transportation, linkages with nursing homes, and community outreach and education are not usually revenue generators alone but they enable providers to build relationships to the community and improve access to inpatient and outpatient services over the long term.

Figure 3.2   Patient Care Continuum

Pre-entry	Acute	Subacute	Outpatient	Home Care
◆ EMS ◆ Nonurgent transportation ◆ Nursing home linkages ◆ Community education and outreach ◆ Prevention/ screening ◆ Web development ◆ Scheduling ◆ Disease management ◆ Information	◆ Critical ◆ Telemetry, stepdown ◆ Routine ◆ Specialty ◆ Long-term acute ◆ 23-hour observation	◆ Skilled nursing ◆ Intermediate ◆ Transitional ◆ Rehabilitation ◆ Respite	◆ Urgent care ◆ Primary care ◆ Specialty care ◆ Diagnostic and treatment ◆ Adult day care ◆ Partial hospitalization ◆ Prevention and wellness	◆ Skilled nursing, home health services ◆ Rehabilitation ◆ Hospice ◆ Assisted living

Note: EMS = emergency medical service.
Source: Health Strategies & Solutions, Inc. 2003. Used with permission.

Other common gaps in the patient care continuum include insufficient critical care and telemetry capacity and inability to care for long-term acute care patients who need a higher level of care than skilled nursing. Changes in the Medicare Prospective Payment System may also make rehabilitation and subacute care services more or less viable than has previously been the case.

Clinical Services Continuum

Service and revenue enhancement opportunities can also be found in the clinical-service-line continuum that includes the range of diagnostic and treatment services for a set of related disorders in clinical areas such as cardiology, oncology, and the neurosciences. Figure 3.3 illustrates the continua for cardiology and oncology. Examining the full range of disorders and treatment modalities within a clinical service line may reveal gaps to be evaluated for potential development.

New medical and surgical treatment modalities continue to expand the cardiology service line. Facilities with large open-heart programs are exploring new surgical techniques such as "beating heart" procedures that avoid use of the heart-lung machine. Community hospitals are initiating

Figure 3.3   Components of a Service Line Continuum

Cardiology Continuum	Oncology Continuum
• Open-heart surgery	• Surgery
• Angioplasty	• Acute inpatient care
• Diagnostic catheterization	• Chemotherapy
• Electrophysiology	• Radiation
• Critical care/telemetry	• Bone-marrow/stem-cell transplants
• Acute care	• Site-specific centers (e.g., breast)
• Diagnostic testing (e.g., MRI, CT scan, ultrasound, stress)	• Health center/resources
	• Diagnostic testing (e.g., radiology, lab/ pathology
• Chest pain	
• Congestive heart failure	• Alternative/complementary medicine
• Rehabilitation	• Hospice
• Wellness/fitness	• Genetic testing
• Clinical protocols/pathways	• Clinical protocols/pathways

Source: Health Strategies & Solutions, Inc. 2003. Used with permission.

invasive cardiology treatment modalities, such as open-heart surgery, now that interventional cardiology has become safer. Technology advances are also spurring a move to use primary angioplasties instead of thrombolytics to treat myocardial infarction.

At the opposite end of the spectrum, many organizations are filling the gap in services available for congestive heart failure (CHF) patients. CHF programs monitor patients and provide dietary and therapeutic interventions. Successful programs can demonstrate improved health status of patients and reduced readmissions and lengths of stay. Although CHF programs are not major revenue generators, they indirectly increase revenue and patients' quality of life.

When scrutinized thoroughly, many clinical service lines will show gaps in services and potential market opportunities. Filling these gaps, whether through internal development or partnering with others, can improve patient care and financial performance.

Develop Niche Services

In the last decade, for-profit healthcare organizations have thrived by employing the niching strategy. These highly innovative and aggressive firms have succeeded by leveraging a narrow type of expertise and concentrating on a specific segment of the care continuum. For-profits employing the niching strategy are most evident in markets where local providers have failed to recognize these opportunities or lacked the focus and attention to provide the high level of service needed to compete in a narrow segment of the market.

Some not-for-profits have now discovered that developing niche services creates revenue growth. These organizations transform parts or all of their organizations to product-line management to facilitate splitting off niches into successful entrepreneurial ventures.

Revenue and services are enhanced when niche services

- create or enhance opportunities to partner with physicians;
- offer a specialty service not otherwise available in a local market;
- possess a high level of expertise and service excellence;
- aim to improve community health; and
- target patient care activities with the potential for positive return.

Figure 3.4 presents a partial list of niche services that offer potential opportunities for many healthcare organizations. Services that are closely aligned with the organization's mission and service capabilities, demonstrate high growth potential, serve unmet community need, and show favorable reimbursement by third party payers will be the most sustainable long term.

Example Niche: Sleep Disorders Center

Many programs in the field of neurosciences show great promise as niche-market opportunities. Several factors influence the growth of neurosciences and the treatment of neurological conditions including the following:

- Increasing incidence of neurology-related conditions due to population aging and the increase in chronic conditions in the elderly
- Increased funding for neurology-related research
- Advances in technology and pharmaceutical interventions
- Growing subspecialization in the neurosciences
- Growing consumer awareness of potential diagnoses and treatments

A large number of people experience sleep disorders, along with headaches, back pain, neuromuscular disorders, cognitive disorders, seizures, and strokes. According to a report by the National Commission on Sleep Disorders Research (1993), at least 40 million Americans have chronic, long-term sleep disorders, while another 20 to 30 million experience occasional problems. The commission estimates that 95 percent of all disorders go undiagnosed, with the most common conditions being insomnia, sleep apnea, restless legs syndrome, and narcolepsy.

Figure 3.4   Potential Niche Services

Medical fitness	Laser surgery
Headache programs	Alzheimer's services
Pain management	School health
Occupational health	Men's reproductive health
Spine centers	Sleep disorders
Complementary/alternative medicine	Lipid centers
Wound care	Sports medicine
International patients	Breast imaging
Diabetes management	Midlife women's centers
Incontinence	Minimally invasive surgery
Geriatrics	Bariatric surgery
Fertility	Congestive heart failure
Aesthetic/cosmetic surgery	

Source: Health Strategies & Solutions, Inc. 2003. Used with permission.

Given the prevalence of chronic sleep conditions, a sleep disorders center can be a niche service that provides a much-needed clinical service and also increases revenues. In addition to contribution margin directly attributable to a sleep disorders center, spin-off volumes for pulmonary function testing, complementary medicine, surgical procedures, pharmaceuticals, and medical equipment may also boost revenues.

In the Northeast, a two-hospital system has operated two sleep labs (one four-bed unit at each hospital) since 1998. This system reports an annual contribution margin of $500,000. A three-hospital system in the Southeast has operated its four-bed sleep lab for 11 years. The annual contribution margin for this single unit is estimated at $1 million.

Clearly as more attention is given to sleep disorders and noticeable growth in demand occurs, hospital-based and freestanding sleep centers and labs become more common. However, other opportunities also exist for providers to distinguish themselves by accreditation status (from the American Academy of Sleep Medicine), strong physician commitment and support, firm commitment from the hospital, and staff certification. Capital costs for equipment (up to $250,000 for two beds) and facility renovations or improvements must be considered, but sleep disorder centers can be successfully deployed and financially rewarding for providers who take the initiative to aggressively seek out opportunities and take swift action when the niche proves to be a viable source of revenue and a needed community service.

Today's successful niches will be followed by even greater variety in the future. Niche-service development is only limited by the marketplace and the imagination of the healthcare organization.

Use Market Segmentation

The final revenue-enhancement strategy is less strategic in nature and instead is driven by marketing. Building on the concepts discussed in Chapter 2, market segmentation is a useful tool for identifying new and expanded approaches for improving services and increasing revenue. By repackaging services and "freshening" them up for specific segments of today's consumer markets, organizations can gain additional business and revenues for existing services with minimal product development or market expansion expenses.

Market segmentation can be subdivided into three categories: demographic segmentation, disease segmentation, and geographic segmentation.

Demographic Segmentation

Demographic segmentation targets services for specific socioeconomic characteristics in patients such as gender, age, or ethnic backgrounds. This patient-focused approach reveals opportunities to improve care through a more targeted or holistic approach to disease management.

Strategies that target women, in particular, are becoming more prevalent. Women influence the vast majority of healthcare decisions made for family members. Women also use services more frequently than men—both physician visits and hospital admissions—and most women are dissatisfied with how they receive care. Organizations employing the market-segmentation strategies can find significant opportunities to develop services for women and even specific age groups of women—services that are distinctive in the marketplace, improve the quality of care, and increase patient satisfaction.

For example, most acute care hospitals have historically defined their strategy for women's healthcare by obstetrical services and little else. More innovative providers now realize that this narrow approach forces hospitals to compete in a highly competitive, poorly reimbursed, and possibly shrinking market. Many organizations find strategies that target a wider spectrum of women's health needs (e.g., perimenopausal care, breast health, bone health, and fitness) provide opportunities to reach and retain female patients for all of their health needs.

Disease Segmentation

Segmenting markets by disease is a useful approach for finding gaps in services and potential sources of revenue. This approach starts with the question, What services are needed by those with a certain condition or disorder?

An assessment of key health status indicators in the service area and a review of high-volume diagnoses admitted or treated by a provider is a good starting point for using disease segmentation. For example, conditions found in an aging population, such as diabetes, arthritis, and heart disease, may be prevalent. Or in some areas, asthma, particularly among children, may be a major health issue.

Once key health issues are confirmed, an inventory of services potentially needed by patients with these conditions can be prepared. An organization then compares this inventory to existing services to locate gaps. For example, if diabetes appears to be a major health issue, a comprehensive diabetes program could coordinate entry into multiple services, such as assessments, weight management, laboratory services, vascular studies, wound care, and other medical and surgical services.

What often becomes evident to providers who undergo these reviews is that they provide most if not all of the services needed to treat a health condition, but the services must be reconfigured to be more patient focused, accessible, and visible to the community.

For some providers, taking their programs to a higher level of clinical and market effectiveness by developing centers of excellence is a valuable opportunity to distinguish themselves in the market. Reorganizing and marketing existing services more productively can significantly improve patient care and create greater market visibility as services are presented in a more comprehensive and integrated fashion. Developing centers of excellence can also move organizations to higher performance levels through patient-centered service enhancements, clinical alignment, integrated operations, outcomes measurement, and focused investments.

Geographic Segmentation

Some regions experiencing significant population growth warrant construction of new acute care facilities to accommodate rapidly increasing demand. A more common occurrence in many communities are pockets of population growth, often on the periphery of existing service areas, that may support additional outpatient services and, over the long term, more acute care capacity.

MAKING REVENUE ENHANCEMENT A TOP ORGANIZATIONAL PRIORITY

During 2001 and 2002, healthcare organizations appeared to find more balance between growth initiatives and cost-reduction measures, rather than being trapped in endless cycles of cost cutting. But many organizations still face the dilemma of making revenue growth a key strategic imperative or moving revenue enhancement projects to the forefront of the many tasks facing healthcare organizations today. Is it possible to make the "good to great" leap that Jim Collins (2001) espouses without growth? Absolutely not! So the question is not whether revenue enhancement should become a top priority, but how and to what degree.

Getting Started

To launch revenue growth as a major organizational initiative or accelerate existing revenue-enhancement measures, two activities must occur. First, an assessment of progress to date must be conducted. The following questions offer a good starting point for identifying issues that should be addressed in the assessment.

- How has revenue changed in the aggregate over the past three years (or longer if desired or required in this and all other areas below)?
- For each major subsidiary or business unit, what are the trends in revenue over the past three years?
- For key programs or services during this period, what is the three-year trend?
- Where in the organization is revenue increasing greatly, and where is it decreasing greatly? Why has this occurred?
- What major growth initiatives have been attempted in the past three years, and with what results?

More detailed questions may be appropriate for some organizations. The goal of the assessment is to come to an understanding about the basis of revenue generation and evaluate the organization's experience and track record with developing new revenue opportunities.

Once this assessment is completed, needs and goals for the next one to three years can be identified. The following questions should be considered when identifying these needs and goals.

- What are the overall and subunit targets for growth for the next one to three years?
- What contribution margin thresholds must new or expanded initiatives meet? What other high-level (e.g., mission-related) factors must be considered, and how?
- To what extent should revenue growth focus on core businesses versus other businesses? How much effort should be directed to new versus expanded programs and services? To new versus existing markets?
- What role should acquisition or strategic alliances play in business development?

Identifying Potential Opportunities

As this chapter has illustrated, a broad range of approaches exist for identifying revenue-enhancement opportunities. To develop a comprehensive list of opportunities that will subsequently be evaluated and ranked, healthcare organizations can employ three activities.

1. *Review the strategic plan and other source documents.* Key documents, such as strategic plans, patient satisfaction surveys, medical staff surveys, market research, and special programmatic studies often reveal opportunities that could be transformed into revenue-generating services.
2. *Conduct a macro analysis.* A macro analysis of the organization and its environment, including material from a strategic plan update or an annual environmental assessment, may help identify additional revenue-producing services.
3. *Gather qualitative input.* Collecting input from sources within and outside of an organization can be a valuable approach for identifying additional opportunities.

It is not unusual for these activities to identify up to 50 (or more in large organizations) opportunities. To keep the process moving forward, it may be necessary to collect more information on each initiative. At the very least, a mini-business plan should be developed for each opportunity.

In some cases, a full-blown feasibility study or business plan may be needed to eliminate the least feasible options and focus on the more promising ones.

Prioritizing Identified Opportunities

Some providers move directly from opportunity identification to implementation. This approach occurs when the need to implement the opportunities seems obvious, an intuitive sense among the leadership about priorities is present, an intense need to move forward exists, or early momentum propels management directly into implementation. However, very few organizations have such compelling reasons to move ahead that would justify skipping the task of prioritizing revenue-enhancement opportunities.

Most organizations will benefit from using a framework to prioritize and rank initiatives. At a minimum, the framework should include consideration of the "fit" of the opportunity with the organization's mission, capabilities, market conditions, and financial situation. In some situations, a much more sophisticated and complex approach is warranted. For example, the financial impact may need to be subdivided into margin, capital needs, risk, and so on, and the criteria weighted.

Once a framework has been created and the prioritization process carried out, a leadership group will typically select the highest-priority initiatives for near-term implementation based on the individual rankings and scores of the revenue-enhancement opportunities.

Implementing High-Priority Opportunities

Providers must resist any temptation to implement too many initiatives at once. Organizations must be realistic about their capacity to manage and sequence a number of activities. The challenge is to maintain organizational enthusiasm and interest even if only a few of the identified opportunities are pursued immediately.

A detailed implementation plan should, at a minimum, include a task listing, assignment of responsibilities, schedule, and summary of significant incremental resources required. In most healthcare organizations, new initiatives are carried out by a primary individual with the support of a few others or a team.

Some organizations struggle with making the transition from planning to implementation, studying opportunities past the point of reason and stalling implementation indefinitely. Others who rush prematurely from planning to implementation may find that the implementation process falters. Experienced managers should be able to judge where and when to transition from planning to implementation.

Once implementation is underway, senior leadership shifts its role to ongoing monitoring, evaluation, and redirecting as needed. Rarely do implementation plans proceed without a hitch. Modifications during implementation are normal, not a sign of flawed planning. Ongoing monitoring and making adjustments when necessary leads to a more successful outcome.

CONCLUSION

By using the five strategies discussed in this chapter to initiate or revive revenue enhancement initiatives, healthcare organizations can break the chronic cycle of cost containment and focus on a future that balances cost control with viable and sustainable revenue-enhancement activities.

NOTE

Much of the content of this chapter previously appeared in a series of articles published by *Health Progress* from March/April 2001 to May/June 2002. The series was written by Alan M. Zuckerman and Tracy K. Johnson.

REFERENCES

American Hospital Association (AHA). 2001. AHA *Hospital Statistics*, 9. Chicago: American Hospital Association and Health Forum.

Broward Regional Health Planning Council, Inc. 2000. *1999 Annual Utilization Report.* Ft. Lauderdale, FL: Broward Regional Health Planning Council.

Collins, J. 2001. *Good to Great: Why Some Companies Make the Leap and Others Don't.* New York: HarperBusiness.

Delaware Valley Healthcare Council. 1999. *Hospital Statistics, 1994–1998.* Philadelphia, PA: Delaware Valley Healthcare Council.

National Commission on Sleep Disorders Research. 1993. "Wake Up America: A National Sleep Alert." Bethesda, MD: National Commission on Sleep Disorders Research/National Institutes of Health.

Zuckerman, A. M., and T. K. Johnson. 2001 "Returning to Revenue Growth." *Health Progress* 82 (2): 19–21, 79.

Chapter 4

Business Development and Program Planning

In the absence of a crystal ball, in fact, a business plan built of the right information and analysis can only be called indispensable.

—*William A. Sahlman (1997)*

OUTSIDE OF HEALTHCARE, developing a business plan is well known as a fundamentally important step for starting a new business or significantly expanding an existing one. Both the quest for excellence and the drive for revenue growth described in the preceding chapter demand this type of business development. Yet it is employed infrequently, inconsistently, and inadequately in healthcare.

Almost endless sources are available to assist in preparing a business plan—books, articles, software packages, easy-to-use templates, and professional business plan writers. There are even annual business plan contests, sponsored by business schools and corporations such as Bank One, Merrill Lynch, and the Harvard Business School, to draw out potential business innovators from universities, hospitals, and research institutions (Entrepreneurs.com 2002).

Stunning examples abound of firms that started with a business plan, including Microsoft, Genentech, and Cisco Systems, and went on to demonstrate amazing success. Is the business plan the reason they succeeded? No one can say for certain, but moving through a rigorous and thoughtful process to create a coherent business plan may have given these organizations the upper hand needed to thrive in today's economy.

While business plans often are viewed as one of the key elements of successful entrepreneurial start-ups, business plans can also revive underperforming organizations. J. Crew was launched in the early 1980s and quickly found its niche by selling Ralph Lauren–style clothes at half the price. Sales grew from $3 million in 1983 to $160 million in 1989. Long-term success proved elusive, however, as high costs, turnover of top-level managers, and tense dynamics among the company's founding family left J. Crew in dire straits by 1997. An innovative new business plan along with a new company president and infusion of capital are credited with making J. Crew one of the strongest clothing businesses in the retail market.

Business plans have even been helpful to nonprofit organizations that typically steer clear of business ventures. Reverend Philip Lance was trying to raise money to support a Latino mission in Los Angeles. His first venture, a thrift shop, was started with a $5,000 donation from the local diocese and $1,000 a month plus donated items from a large Beverly Hills congregation (*Forbes* 1998). The store was quickly taking in $15,000 a month. Lance's next venture was not so successful. His household-help business charged clients $8.50 per hour for various chores, but Lance failed to factor in the costs of liability insurance and workers' compensation costs, and the company was soon losing money. A business course helped Lance develop a business plan for a janitorial service that allows employees to become owners of the business. The company, whose 16 employees now have adequate insurance, make up to $7.50 per hour with paid vacation, and company revenues have hit $33,000 per month (*Forbes* 1998).

RATIONALES FOR DEVELOPING A BUSINESS PLAN

Given the great importance attached to developing a business plan, organizations often jump into developing a plan without taking the important step of reviewing why a business plan is actually needed.

Six primary reasons may exist for developing a business plan.

1. *Outside funding is needed.* Obtaining the support of lenders or investors requires more than a seemingly good idea. Lenders or investors will demand a thoughtful, detailed rationale and plan before committing to support the new or expanded venture and then will monitor progress as the plan goes forward.
2. *Internal approvals and funding are required.* In large corporations, approvals and funding may be necessary to get a new or expanded

initiative off the ground in one part of their business. In some corporations, multiple approvals may be required as the proposed venture passes through different levels of the organizational bureaucracy. The approval processes may have varying requirements for the level of detail included in the business plan.

3. *External approvals are required.* Depending on the nature of the initiative, one or more external bodies may have a say in whether or how the initiative proceeds. Typical approval bodies are local, state, or federal governmental authorities that exercise regulatory or licensing authority over some aspect of the proposed venture.

4. *The plan facilitates internal consensus building.* In the absence of a business plan, it is usually unclear how feasible or desirable the proposed venture is. The business plan helps to build the case for proceeding, defines and describes expectations for outcomes, and assists in bringing various internal leadership elements together on key features and outcomes of business development.

5. *Business plans expedite and save money on capital expansion and subsequent operations.* A new or expanded venture often will involve some capital expansion. A clear, detailed business plan may help fast-track capital development, saving both time and money. A good business plan can jump-start operations, with operational planning occurring well in advance of the start or establishment date in anticipation of future needs.

6. *Secondary issues are identified and potentially resolved with a business plan.* Many times, developing the new or expanded venture itself is a fairly straightforward proposition or at least is bounded, definable, and manageable. However, secondary or related issues and their associated effects may crop up and delay, derail, or disable the venture. A good business plan anticipates and addresses secondary issues before they appear and cripple or block the initiative.

COMPONENTS AND CHARACTERISTICS OF AN EFFECTIVE BUSINESS PLAN

William Sahlman (1997), a professor at Harvard Business School, believes that most business plans overemphasize the numbers and fail to cover the information that investors really want to see. Most financial projections, especially those that project past the first year, are an act of imagination. Sahlman (1997) advises that numbers should appear in a business plan primarily in the form of a business model to demonstrate that key drivers of the venture's success or failure have been thoroughly evaluated. He suggests using the following framework.

- *The people*: the staff who will start and run the venture and any outside parties or resources that will be used (e.g., lawyers, accountants, suppliers, etc.)
- *The opportunity*: a profile of the business, including what it will sell or provide and to whom, the economics involved, and who and what could prevent success
- *The context*: details about the regulatory environment, interest rates, demographic trends, and other factors that cannot be controlled by the entrepreneurs
- *Risk and reward*: an assessment of everything that could go right and wrong and a discussion of approaches for responding to these possibilities

Rich and Gumpert (1985) note that one of the fundamentals most frequently overlooked in business plans is the accurate reflection of the viewpoints of three key constituencies: the market (existing and prospective clients), investors (financial or other resources), and the producer (the entrepreneur or inventor). Rich and Gumpert argue that too many business plans focus on the viewpoint of the producer and neglect the market and investor perspectives necessary to give the venture its financial viability.

They cite a case of five executives seeking financing to establish their own engineering consulting firm. Their business plan listed a dozen specialized engineering services and estimated their annual sales and profit growth at 20 percent. The executives failed to note which of the services their clients really needed and which would be the most profitable and ignored the possibility that the market might want services not included in the business plan. The investors' perspective was also ignored. The price of the new shares and the percentage available to investors was not specified. Because the plan only focused on the producer's perspective it lacked the credibility needed to raise investment funds. Rich and Gumpert (1985) advise: "Write your business plan by looking outward to your key constituencies rather than looking inward at what suits you best. You will save valuable time and energy this way and improve your chances of winning investors and customers."

FOUR KEY QUALITIES

What constitutes an effective business plan? The following four qualities are especially important:

1. *Completeness.* As described later in this chapter, there is a minimum scope that the business plan must encompass, and many funding or approval bodies are explicitly or implicitly aware of content requirements. Failure to address a standard element of the business plan may render it unacceptable. Failure to address a standard element in sufficient depth is another fatal mistake.
2. *Rigor.* Parties reviewing the plan will expect a certain level of rigor in the analyses that underlie and appear in the business plan. In particular, the market and financial analyses should be analytically sound and thorough.
3. *Input.* Business plans are often scrutinized for the completeness and thoroughness of the input gathered during plan development. Evidence of appropriate internal and external data and information collection and interaction with or feedback from key affected parties may influence the perception of whether sufficient input was provided in the business planning process.
4. *Readability.* The business plan must be comprehensible, well written, and easy to read, yet many business plans fail to meet these basic requirements. Large corporations often provide internal support to their managers and technical staff to assist them in creating readable business plans and other documents. Consultants abound to provide such assistance to those not fortunate enough to have internal staff support.

BUSINESS PLANNING IN HEALTHCARE TODAY

Business planning is still in its nascent stage in healthcare delivery. On the nonprofit side, up until the 1990s, the availability of fairly easy money, a wealth of opportunities, small and unsophisticated organizations, and neither internal leadership nor external approval-body demands necessitated the type of business planning common outside of healthcare. However, the bar has been raised considerably by the tightening financial environment; the growth of large, complex healthcare networks and systems; and the increasingly frequent and highly publicized financial difficulties experienced by some healthcare organizations.

In contrast, however, in for-profit healthcare, business planning is common and prevalent. Since nearly all for-profits are relatively new start-up companies—their histories rarely extend back prior to 1990—without internal resources to support and sustain them, a compelling business case was required to gain the financial support of investors and get new ventures off the ground.

The typical path of for-profits in healthcare is to start as a private corporation, with some combination of internal lender, selected investors, and/or venture capital support. The venture may then later transition to a publicly held corporation through a stock offering. In essentially all cases, a business plan is required initially to secure external funding and then subsequent modifications and updates to the business plan are executed later as the organization becomes operational, develops, and then goes public.

Salick Health Care illustrates this typical path of for-profit start-ups in healthcare. Dr. Bernard Salick, a nephrologist who pioneered the idea of 24-hour kidney dialysis centers, believed this concept would translate well to outpatient cancer treatment. His ideas were solidified when his daughter was diagnosed with cancer and had difficulties scheduling her chemotherapy regimens during traditional offices hours. Salick envisioned a full continuum of high-quality, patient-centered oncology services available in a single facility 24 hours a day and 7 days a week.

Armed with a solid business plan and a vision for a new approach to cancer care that would eventually change how the entire industry approaches management of chronic diseases, Salick proceeded to establish 11 full-service cancer centers in California, New York, and Florida, some in partnership with leading hospitals, systems, and a network of over 100 physicians. His centers offered insurers a fixed-price menu of services. At a time when no other provider would accept a cap, he would treat for a single premium any enrolled patient who developed cancer (France 1998).

Modifications to the centers and their services have been made as the businesses were put into operation. For example, the architecture at the Salick center at Cedars-Sinai Medical Center in Los Angeles was judged to be too harsh as Salick attempted to move away from the notion of creating a soothing domestic environment in patient care areas. Design flaws also led to patients in hospital gowns sitting in the same waiting room with clothed patients and their families.

The businesses performed well financially, going public in 1985 with the help of Drexel Burnham Lambert. Even when accepting patients with the most insidious cases of cancer, the centers were able to control costs and build attractive profit margins by minimizing the need for hospitalizations. In 1997, Salick sold his chain of cancer centers to the Zeneca Group, a British pharmaceutical corporation, for $480 million (France 1998).

HEALTHCARE NONPROFITS RECOGNIZE THE VALUE OF BUSINESS PLANNING

More recently, healthcare not-for-profits are recognizing the value of business planning. When MCG Health, Inc. (Augusta, Georgia) was formed in 2000 to integrate the clinical enterprises of the Medical College of Georgia (hospital, clinics, and faculty practices), a series of business plans were developed to chart a course for key clinical programs within the organization. These plans were intended to guide future development and resource allocations as well as marshal internal support for emphasis on certain clinical directions. Beginning with neurosciences, and then followed shortly by oncology and cardiovascular services, MCG Health leadership developed the business case and underlying rationale to coordinate and then significantly expand and enhance its services in these three key clinical areas.

Washoe Health System in Reno, Nevada, was considering developing a neurosciences institute in 2001 but was unsure whether, and if so, how, to proceed. The system already had a strong regional position in basic neurology and neurosurgery and fairly large and interested groups of neurologists and neurosurgeons who believed that a program of regional excellence could and should be developed. But significant additional investments would be required to create an integrated, truly distinctive neurosciences center. The business plan Washoe Health System developed with its neurosciences staff details the case for establishing a neurosciences institute in a phased, financially prudent manner and is serving as a clear road map for leadership to follow during implementation.

ESSENTIAL COMPONENTS OF A TYPICAL BUSINESS PLAN

Figure 4.1 illustrates the typical contents of a business plan. The eight components shown in the diagram, and the subcomponents of each,

Figure 4.1   What's in a Business Plan?

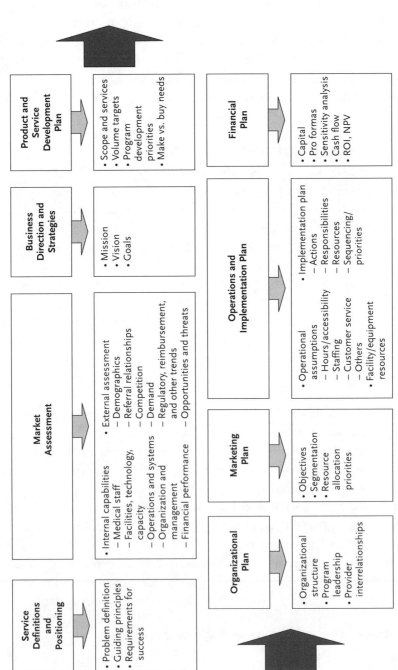

Note: ROI = return on investment; NPV = net present value.
Source: Health Strategies & Solutions, Inc. 2003. Used with permission.

collectively constitute a minimum amount of content for a standard business plan. The flow, in terms of plan development and presentation, typically proceeds from left to right and top to bottom in the diagram, beginning with service definitions and positioning and ending with the financial plan. The business plan usually has a three- to five-year time frame, although it may reference longer-term development and specify some aspects of the near-term development in great detail.

The only additional standard business plan component not shown is an executive summary. The executive summary is a one- to two-page (maximum) high-level statement of overall findings and recommendations.

The amount of time required to complete most business plans ranges from three to six months. This time frame provides enough time to carry out the work required and obtain sufficient input and other participation in the process to ensure thorough consideration of all elements of the business plan. The pages that follow describe each of the business plan components in more detail.

Services Definitions and Positioning

The first component, service definitions and positioning, may seem so clear cut that little text or analysis is needed—and in many cases this is so. However, many more situations exist where the business venture in question is not commonly understood by all, either internally or externally. For instance, in a cardiac business plan, is the subject medical cardiology and cardiac surgery alone, or does it include thoracic services, vascular services, or both? Is it confined to adult care, pediatric care, or both? In an oncology business plan, does it include medical, radiation, and surgical care? If not, what components are in or out? In healthcare, the coverage of a business plan is rarely obvious to all.

The business plan may also need to clarify at the outset how the program is expected to be positioned in the market—niche versus full service, high end versus low end, academic versus purely clinical. Key principles that will guide clinical program development (e.g., growth orientation, brand identity, innovation, etc.) may also require discussion in the plan (see Figure 4.2).

When completing this part of the business plan, it is important to clearly articulate the business that the organization is proposing to develop or expand: What problem or need does the business address? What are the overall organizational principles or tenets that will guide

---

Figure 4.2   Sample Guiding Principles for Clinical Program Development

- Clarity of program vision and strategic direction
- Clinical excellence and innovation
- Full range of diagnostic and treatment services
- Dedicated administrative and physician "champions"
- Multidisciplinary team(s) of providers
- Operational and clinical coordination
- Demonstrated superior quality
- Strong growth orientation
- Focused marketing and distinctive brand identity
- Commitment to education and clinical research

Source: Health Strategies & Solutions, Inc. 2003. Used with permission.

---

business development? What will constitute a successful endeavor after the plan is executed?

Market Assessment

The second component, market assessment, is probably most familiar to healthcare planners and managers since it is a common part of many strategic plans, feasibility studies, and program analyses conducted in the field. Figure 4.3 illustrates an example of the typical summary output of the market assessment—the strengths, weaknesses, opportunities, and threats analysis (SWOT).

What may be different in the business plan market assessment are the requirements for analytical rigor and focus. The market assessment is not meant to be a general environmental scan, but rather sharply focused on the business in question. The business plan must carefully and clearly define the relevant market for the venture and analyze what capabilities and shortfalls the organization has in relation to the market opportunity. In the for-profit world, the market is sized and segmented, and external forces affecting future market characteristics and their impacts are described and analyzed. Competitors are inventoried and analyzed, and their strategies in relation to the market must be assessed and compared to determine opportunities to exploit competitor weaknesses.

The product of the market assessment is a quantitative and qualitative profile of the market, both current and future, for the business venture

Figure 4.3   Example Market Assessment Summary: SWOT Analysis for Cardiovascular Program

STRENGTHS	WEAKNESSES
◆ Scope of services ◆ Teaching program ◆ Basic sciences research ◆ Regional draw	◆ Program size and market position ◆ Inadequate capacity to accommodate growth (e.g., one cath lab) ◆ Supporting services (screening, prevention, education, etc.) ◆ Payer mix ◆ Reputation as indigent care hospital ◆ Lack of clinical research ◆ Lack of program infrastructure

OPPORTUNITIES	THREATS
◆ Partnerships for "quick hits" to volume (e.g., VA, prison system) ◆ Differentiate on quality ◆ Facility enhancements to improve accessibility and patient flow ◆ New service development (e.g., chest pain center, transplant program) ◆ Clinical research efforts ◆ Recruitment and referral network development	◆ Local market competition at cutthroat levels ◆ Regional market opportunities potentially blocked by strong competitors in nearby markets ◆ Potential sunset of certificate of need could intensify competition for some services ◆ Payer mix ◆ Loss of additional pediatric volume

Source: Health Strategies & Solutions, Inc. 2003. Used with permission.

in question. If the business venture is to succeed, the market assessment must delineate clear opportunities for volume capture in many or all of the proposed services.

Business Direction and Strategies

The third component, business direction and strategies, frames the overall challenge for business development in the following terms.

- *Mission.* What is the fundamental purpose of the business the organization is in or entering? What does the business do, and who does it intend to serve?
- *Vision.* What does the organization want the business to be in the distant future (approximately ten years)? What distinctive characteristics or qualities should the business have in its future state? What is a future state that the business should aspire to? What future state represents a desirable stretch from the current situation

and will be perceived as motivational for key employees and other stakeholders?
- *Goals.* What intermediate (approximately three to five years) targets should be set to help the business progress toward its vision?

The mission, vision, and goals create the context for moving the new or expanded initiative forward in the short term. Answering the question "Where are we going?" establishes long-term direction for the business, creates a road map, and illuminates a path for the rest of the business plan.

Direction can be expressed in a variety of ways to provide appropriate guidance. Size, scope, geography, societal or population-specific benefits, and the like are commonly used in the direction element by healthcare organizations (see, e.g., business plan goals in Figure 4.4).

Product and Service Development Plan

The fourth component, the product and service development plan, begins the transition of the business plan from concept to reality. At this point, opportunities identified in earlier tasks become tangible aspects of the new or expanded initiative.

A central element of the product and service development plan is a clear statement of the scope of services to be provided and any phased implementation of services. In most cases, service development will be phased in over a multiyear period. Figures 4.5 and 4.6 illustrate these critical concepts and delineate the full scope of services of a neuroscience center and a phased service development plan for a women's health program.

Volume targets constitute another critical aspect of the product and service development plan. These targets should express the size of demands for each service over time as the business grows and develops. The volume forecasts offer important input to the staffing model and revenue projections that are developed later. The volume targets should link to identified program development priorities and provide a quantitative expression of aspects of the program to be emphasized over others.

Lastly, consideration should be given to "home grown" service development versus that which is purchased, subcontracted, or carried out through some type of strategic alliance with others. Historically, healthcare organizations have preferred to go it alone, while the partnering model is far more common in other industries.

Figure 4.4   Illustrative Business Plan Goals

Goals describe general ends toward which the program will direct its efforts
for the next three to five years

- **Enhanced Scope and Organization of Services:** More specialized capabili-
  ties and enhanced coordination of care
- **Volume and Revenue Growth:** Dominant local provider and greater
  regional draw
- **Superior Quality:** Favorable clinical outcomes, robust clinical research
- **Sustainable Cost Position:** Adequate margin for future program development investments
- **Leadership:** Dedicated administrative and clinical leaders aggressively
  "championing" program development efforts
- **Employee Satisfaction:** Status as the employer of choice for well-trained,
  service-oriented clinical and support staff
- **Brand Identity:** Aggressive marketing strategy that results in a distinctive
  brand identity

Source: Health Strategies & Solutions, Inc. 2003. Used with permission.

Organizational Plan

The fifth component, the organizational plan, addresses how the business
will organize to deliver the scope of services. In an existing business, change
in the organizational structure may be required to move forward according
to the business plan outline developed in the preceding activities. In a
multi-entity corporation (i.e., a healthcare system or any large, complex
organization), the business unit structure must be consistent and integrate
with other comparable, supporting and supervisory structures. Organizational structures for clinical programs, especially in large organizations, may
be quite complex, as the example shown in Figure 4.7 illustrates.

A key element of the organizational plan is business leadership.
Healthcare businesses increasingly seek to identify physician leaders to
head important units, sometimes solely and other times in conjunction
with nonphysician managers. This dual structure is very common in hospitals, where, historically, clinical departments have had medical and
nonmedical leaders. In the increasingly difficult financial environment

Figure 4.5   Sample Neuroscience Disease-Specific Centers

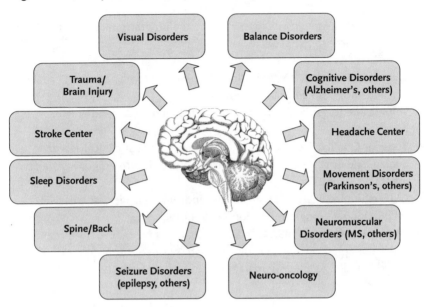

Source: Health Strategies & Solutions, Inc. 2003. Used with permission.

facing most healthcare organizations, strong financial skills are often a must for business unit leaders.

Finally, healthcare businesses frequently involve complex provider interrelationships that should be given explicit consideration at the outset. Issues often emerge relative to the various roles and responsibilities of participating physicians and the general medical staff. If alternatives such as purchasing components, subcontracting items, or establishing strategic alliances with outside groups to deliver some aspects of the program are pursued, organizational relationships warrant careful consideration and specification to clarify roles and responsibilities from the outset.

Marketing Plan

The sixth component, the marketing plan, begins to translate the scope of service needs and volume forecasts into operational reality. While the product and service development plan describes the "what" of the business (services, scope, how much, priorities), the marketing plan describes "how" the service volumes will be achieved.

Figure 4.6   Sample Program Development Priorities: Women's Health Program

Immediate Priorities (1–2 Years)	Second Round Priorities (3–5 Years)	Potential Future Priorities for Consideration
◆ Maternal/child ◆ Gynecology (surgery and gyn oncology, etc.) ◆ Breast care ◆ Incontinence/ urogynecology ◆ Bone and joint health (osteoporosis, sports, orthopedics, etc.) ◆ To be cross-marketed/packaged with senior health ◆ Pain (e.g., fibromyalgia, lymphedema, cancer)	◆ Depression ◆ Domestic violence ◆ Diabetes ◆ Cardiovascular ◆ Pending cardiac strategy ◆ Women's digestive diseases (e.g., irritable bowel syndrome)	◆ Cosmetic surgery ◆ Dermatology ◆ Eating disorders ◆ Headache ◆ Sports medicine

Source: Health Strategies & Solutions, Inc. 2003. Used with permission.

The marketing component of a business plan is usually not a full marketing plan for the venture, but it does provide sufficient detail on how to realize the business objectives. It typically segments the market into various target subcomponents by geography, age, sex, or other commonly used measures. The plan outlines strategies to cultivate each segment and may also describe the various marketing media and tactics necessary to carry out the strategies. The example in Figure 4.8 illustrates the scope and level of detail required in the marketing plan element of the business plan.

An overall image or identity program may be required to carry out the marketing plan effectively. Also, the marketing program may need to be coordinated with and linked to other marketing initiatives within the organization.

Marketing of new or greatly expanded services typically entails significant resources. The level of funding required in the first few years of implementation of the business plan is often a carefully scrutinized output of this process. An important consideration may be the human marketing capital, as represented by the time commitment to carry out various aspects of the marketing plan.

Figure 4.7   Sample Organization—Proposed Clinical Structure

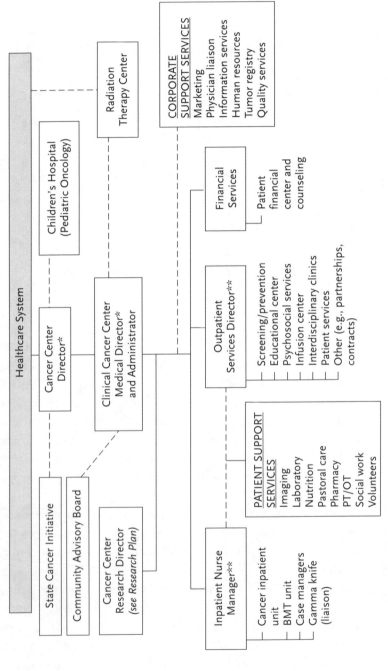

* Could be combined initially

** Nursing personnel also report to CNO

Source: Health Strategies & Solutions, Inc. 2003. Used with permission.

Figure 4.8　Sample Marketing Plan: Bloodless Medicine/Surgery

Target Market Segment	Action	Resource Requirements (1)	Target Time Frame (2)	Responsibility
Jehovah's Witnesses	◆ Develop a closer relationship with the local Witness community 　–Participate in local events, as appropriate 　–Meet with local leaders on a regular basis to share information and address any concerns regarding bloodless program	Low	Short term	Program coordinators and program leader
	◆ Showcase the medical staff experience, philosophy, and participation in the advancements of bloodless techniques	Low	Short term	Program leader
	◆ Enhance patient information and education resources on hospital and bloodless programs 　–On-site library (e.g., videos, brochures) 　–Focus groups 　–Speaker's bureau	Low to Medium	Short term	Program coordinator and executive staff
	◆ Promote clinical outcomes and use of new technologies	Low	Short to Medium term	Medical Advisory Board
	◆ Develop collaborative relationships with established bloodless programs nationally	Low	Short to Medium term	Program coordinators and Medical Advisory Board
	◆ Incorporate bloodless program description into hospital web site; link page to related sites on Internet	Medium to High	Medium to Long term	Program leader
Local "non-Witness" population	◆ Sponsor programs tailored to specific populations	Low	Short term	Program coordinators
	◆ Target program in hospital's regular communications (e.g., newsletters)	Low	Short term	Program leader
Physicians	◆ Promote clinical research, presentations, and publications to referring physicians, especially nonaffiliated	Medium	Medium term	Medical Advisory Board
Payers	◆ Promote highly specialized services as regional center of excellence	Medium	Medium term	CFO
	◆ Market as a cost-effective alternative to regular surgery	Low	Medium term	CFO
	◆ Market as an area of distinction for hospital	Low	Medium term	CFO
	◆ Promote clinical research, presentations, and publications	Medium	Medium term	CFO

(1) **Low** = 0–10 person days and/or an incremental amount of <$10,000 per year
Medium = 10–20 person days and/or an incremental amount of $10,000–$20,000 per year
High = 20+ person days and/or an incremental amount of >$20,000 per year

(2) **Short term** = within six months
Medium term = within 12 months
Long term = within 18–24 months

Source: Health Strategies & Solutions, Inc. 2003. Used with permission.

Operations and Implementation Plan

The seventh component, the operations and implementation plan, is another important bridge from planning to actualization of the business plan. Here, many of the critical assumptions that dictate how the business will operate are specified, and a framework for proceeding with implementation is outlined. This component also provides important input for the eighth and final component of the business plan, the financial plan.

The operations plan's purpose is to provide sufficient detail on how the business will operate to allow operational and financial feasibility to be determined. It is not intended to be a full operational or policies and procedures manual, although these may be prepared subsequently. The operations plan should cover key areas such as hours of operation; number, type, and qualifications of staff required; and customer service standards.

Often, business development involves significant capital expenditures for facilities and major equipment. Where this is envisioned, the nature and magnitude of expenditures required by category, along with the supporting rationale, should be provided in the business plan.

Lastly, concurrent with financial plan preparation, an implementation plan that allows the venture to move forward expeditiously must be developed. Typically, the implementation plan is very detailed for the next 12 to 18 months (see example in Figure 4.9) and more general after that. At a minimum, the implementation plan should include key actions and associated individual and group responsibilities, incremental capital and operating resources required, and a schedule for carrying out each action.

Financial Plan

The eighth and final component of the business plan is the financial plan. This plan demonstrates the financial feasibility of pursuing the new or expanded initiative over a three- to five-year period. If financial feasibility cannot be shown, it is unlikely the venture will be pursued. It is not unusual to develop multiple iterations of the financial plan, as assumptions are revised to increase the likelihood of good financial performance of the venture.

There are two subcomponents of the financial plan, the capital and operating plans. The capital plan includes definition of needs for and potential sources of capital required to carry out the venture. Potential outside sources of funding, at least by category, should be identified, along with likely major terms and conditions of obtaining outside funding and implications for operating performance. Operational financial

Figure 4.9 Sample Implementation Plan to Address Western Region Oncology Program

GOAL: Moderate growth to recoup recent losses and begin to increase market share (e.g., PSA new cancer case market share > 21%; RT market share > 11%)
PROJECTED IMPLEMENTATION COST: $1,700,000+

Objectives and Action Steps	Resource Requirements (1) and Priority Level	Target Completion (2)	Responsibility (3)
01: Consistent with system overall strategy, leverage breast and other women's cancer services A1: Maximize benefit from transition of Dr. S's practice A2: Arrange for complementary services to be provided at same site as Dr. S A3: Consider developing lymphedema services and (consider) a partnership with Tristate lymphedema clinic	N/A (accounted for elsewhere) and high priority	Short term and ongoing	Program administrator and COO
02: Recruit university-affiliated and other oncology subspecialties A1: Follow up on interest expressed by ENT physician (w/significant cancer component) to move practice to hospital A2: Follow up on interest expressed by hematologist to move his practice to hospital	Minimal and high priority	Short term and ongoing	Program administrator and COO
03: Further penetrate west side A1: Strengthen ties with affiliated PCPs on the west side and recruit new PCPs A2: Develop targeted marketing and outreach programs A3: Provide lymphedema services and make other services available at new MOB	Minimal and high priority	Short term and ongoing	Physician administrator, physician services, and corp. communications
04: Enhance primary care base by strengthening existing relationships with PCPs and developing new relationships A1: Develop closer working relationships with PCPs; recruit new PCPs for existing/new sites A2: Identify reasons why service area patients are referred to other programs and address as necessary A3: Facilitate communication and assist in strengthening relationships between PCPs and oncologists (put together brochures and information packets for PCPs)	Minimal and medium priority	Short term and ongoing	Physician services
05: Make hospital more efficient and attractive for physicians to practice A1: Solicit feedback from physicians on existing operational strengths and weaknesses A2: Identify operational deficiencies and address as necessary	TBD and medium priority	Medium term and ongoing	Program administrator and COO
06: Promote/take advantage of capabilities in high-dose radiation A1: Promote service generally A2: Utilize Dr. G in promotional activities	Minimal and medium priority	Short term and ongoing	Program administrator and corp. communications
07: Continue to upgrade equipment A1: Replace 4/6 linear accelerator with new unit A2: Develop a plan to replace the 8/20 dual energy (with electrons) linear accelerator early FY 2002 A3: Replace 8/20 linear accelerator with MLC technology early FY 2002	Significant and high priority	Short-term/medium term	Program administrator

(1) Direct resource requirements—Reflects the magnitude of incremental resources ($ amount and/or level of effort) required to achieve this objective; Excludes resource requirements for related goals and objectives. Significant, 1.0 + FTE or $100,000+; moderate, .5 to 1.0 FTE or $50,000 to $100,000; minimal, less than .5 FTE or $50,000.

(2) Target completion—Short term, 0 to 12 months; Medium term, 12 to 36 months; Long term 36+ months

(3) Responsibility—Individual(s) leading effort and accountable for successful completion of the objective.

Source: Health Strategies & Solutions, Inc. 2003. Used with permission.

forecasts, termed financial pro formas, cover the key revenue and expense categories and important underlying assumptions. Both operating and cash flow statements are traditionally prepared.

As noted above, multiple iterations of the financial forecasts are the norm in business planning, which ultimately results in consensus on a final forecast. At the outset—and sometimes later—sensitivity analyses, demonstrating the effects of changes in key variables (e.g., volume higher or lower, increased/decreased debt, etc.) are prepared to help inform the analysis and discussion of potential futures. The product of the sensitivity analyses as applied to the projected future income statement is illustrated by the example in Figure 4.10.

Finally, the financial plan typically concludes by displaying projected financial performance relative to comparable norms using a variety of standard measures, such as return on investment and net present value, to demonstrate that the venture meets certain thresholds for satisfactory (or better) financial performance.

PROCESS NEEDS FOR EFFECTIVE BUSINESS PLANNING

This chapter thus far has addressed the content needs for an effective business plan. This section describes some of the process considerations in business planning, including oversight and direction, input, and review and approval.

Oversight and Direction

Oversight and direction of the business planning process is usually the responsibility of both an individual and a group. A lead person is needed to take principal responsibility for managing the business plan development process. Typically, a steering committee is created composed of individuals involved in the affected business and others who may have a broader role in the business unit's division or company.

Healthcare often involves aspects of oversight and direction not found in other businesses. It is not unusual to need multiple levels of oversight and direction—from a management group, a physician group, and a board group, or some combination of the above for the business planning process. The occasional temptation to vest responsibility for day-to-day management of the business planning process in at least two individuals—a manager and a physician or other clinician or sometimes a small and other times large multidisciplinary committee—should be resisted because accountability is clearest when a single individual is responsible.

Figure 4.10 Projected Impact of Adult Cardiovascular Center of Excellence Strategies on Cardiovascular Product Line Financial Performance, by Scenario, FY 2005[1]

Year - Scenario	Net Revenue	Direct Expenses	Program Margin	Incremental Program Margin from FY 2000 - Baseline	Incremental Infrastructure Operating Costs from Baseline	Incremental Contribution Margin
FY 2000 - Baseline	$ 30,792,810	$ 18,193,742	$ 12,599,068	N/A	N/A	N/A
FY 2005 - Maintain share	$ 37,568,934	$ 22,208,814	$ 15,360,120	$ 2,761,053	$ 1,090,000	$ 1,671,053
FY 2005 - Moderate growth	$ 48,829,221	$ 28,892,150	$ 19,937,071	$ 7,338,004	$ 1,090,000	$ 6,248,004
FY 2005 - Aggressive growth	$ 59,680,598	$ 35,332,732	$ 24,347,866	$ 11,748,799	$ 1,090,000	$ 10,658,799
FY 2005 - Decline	$ 26,773,587	$ 15,799,253	$ 10,974,333	$ (1,624,734)	$ 1,090,000	$ (2,714,734)

(1) Based on adult hospital cardiovascular patients and cardiology clinic patients. Requires a five-year total capital investment of approximately $3,670,000 (preliminary estimate). Average annual return on investment through FY 2005 = 26%.

Source: Health Strategies & Solutions, Inc. 2003. Used with permission.

Input

Similarly, the amount of input required or desired is generally far more extensive in healthcare than in other industries. At a minimum, individual and group input is necessary to understand the market and to provide technical support for completion of each of the subcomponent plans—product, organizational, marketing, operations, and financial. Outside of healthcare, this input is generally accomplished in a straightforward manner by consulting knowledgeable individuals and groups as necessary.

In healthcare, much more input is sought and the processes to gather it are often far more extensive. Many individuals and groups are likely to be solicited for input on the market and development of the subcomponent plans. Formal or informal task forces may be established to advise on the development of the marketing and financial plans, in particular, and sometimes other components. Depending on the organization, process requirements may vary from fairly minimal to incredibly extensive. The scope of process requirements will have a significant effect on both the time frame needed to complete the plan and the staff time involved in carrying out the planning process.

Review and Approval

The review and approval process also varies depending on the number of levels of oversight and the complexity of the organization. At a minimum, the business planning steering committee provides the first level of review and approval, generally recommending the business plan for approval to higher levels. In most healthcare organizations today it is the norm for a senior management group to provide a second level of review before a board committee or the board itself provides the final review and ultimate approval. For nonresource-intensive plans or in narrowly focused areas, it is not unusual for the senior management team and/or the chief executive officer to have final approval authority. For highly resource-intensive plans or ones with a very broad scope, additional review and approval steps may be required. In the latter case, some type of review could be desirable or required by a medical staff group or the finance committee of the board.

OPERATIONS PLANNING, ROLLOUT, AND START-UP

Once the plan is approved, in nearly all cases a variety of activities will need to be carried out before commencement of full operations. In these situations, planning shifts from proving that developing a business is viable to preparing to operate that business.

Operations Planning

Depending on the nature of the business, operations planning may be focused on extending and enhancing an existing line of business or starting from scratch to develop a new line. Also, in some situations in an existing line, the business plan may call for extensive changes in operations. Obviously, the extent of change in operations dictates how extensive and time consuming the planning will be for the new/expanded operation.

Following completion of the business plan, construction may be necessary, and major, expensive equipment may need to be procured. In these situations, operations planning may take a back seat to capital funds development, facility planning, design and construction, review of equipment options and bids, and purchase and installation of equipment. In some cases, however, the capital expansion process is so consuming that operations planning never formally commences or does not occur until operations begin—both of which are enormous mistakes with significant consequences in nearly all cases. Operations policies, processes, and systems will need to be overhauled at a minimum, and the time from business plan approval to commencement of operations is the best time to give this issue full and careful consideration. In a new business, failure to use this time for operations planning could well be fatal to the new operation.

Rollout

In most cases, three to six months before full operations begin, the emphasis moves from operations planning to the rollout phase. At this time, staff recruitment and hiring commences; marketing moves into a plan finalization and then activation stage; and, as D-day nears, testing of new operational policies, procedures, and systems begins, along with pre-start debugging of operations. The rollout phase ends with the organization or unit ready to go live as a result of a smooth transition from planning to initial operations.

Start-Up

The start-up phase begins during the month prior to commencing full operations and lasts into the first few months of operation. The transition from planning to putting the venture into operation should be relatively seamless, with the organization or unit ready to greet and treat patients as they arrive. Usually, phase-in to full operations takes place over the first few weeks or months of new operations, with additional capacity and services brought online gradually during the phase-in period. This approach also allows the organization to test and revise its operational processes and systems to accommodate the scope of services and volume of patient demands in a planned manner. This approach significantly diminishes the possibility of being overwhelmed and unable to perform effectively in the first few days and weeks of operations.

The start-up phase is a period of extensive debugging of operations. The goal is to have full capacity online, with effective operations, as soon as possible after start-up, although not necessarily on day one and not in a rushed manner that compromises the chances of success in six months or a year after start-up.

FOSTERING ENTREPRENEURIALISM AND LEADERSHIP

Business plan development and implementation is usually driven and guided by one or more interested, responsible individuals. While organizations can and often do identify many great opportunities to pursue, in the absence of individual entrepreneurs and leaders, it becomes impossible to realize the opportunities. Sometimes these leaders can be recruited into the organization after the business plan is complete or as the venture is being put into operation. Ultimately, the success of the venture depends heavily on the individual(s) directing the business unit and the magnitude of the opportunity available.

There is no substitute for the energy and drive that entrepreneurial leaders bring to new or significantly expanded businesses. During this high-growth stage, it is critical to have at least one person in a position of responsibility who excels at business development. An entrepreneur takes on the business development challenge as a single-minded pursuit, with a passion and commitment that managers of mature businesses rarely have. Entrepreneurialism is a highly desired quality in the development, start-up, and high-growth, early phases. Successful entrepreneurs usually grow restless when the business enters a more mature phase of operations and are rarely good managers and leaders in a slow-growth or maintenance mode.

In healthcare, having entrepreneurial physicians and clinicians—in addition to entrepreneurial managers—involved in start-ups or expansions is the optimal situation. These clinical entrepreneurs will push the envelope in a way lay entrepreneurs will not or cannot and have a synergistic effect, spurring high growth.

Business and management research on the subject of entrepreneurialism suggests that entrepreneurs are born, not made. If business unit leaders are not entrepreneurial and new entrepreneurial staff are not brought in from the outside, this spark is likely to remain lacking in the organization or unit.

Equally important to business success are leadership skills and talents. The challenge of leadership in an emerging business line is significant and quite different than that of a more mature business. Paramount in the early stages of business development is the ability to

- shape and motivate the organization or unit to grow toward stretch goals;
- develop additional capacities and resources as necessary in the high-growth times;
- stabilize and support the organization or unit as it navigates through shaky financial times toward profitability and viability; and
- guide and direct the organization/unit in the developmental phase.

Unlike entrepreneurialism, it is possible to develop and refine leadership skills at least to some degree. Managers or manager candidates in new or expanding business units would be wise to seek such training and education to sharpen their skills and increase their effectiveness.

Finally, when business units reach a mature phase, the leadership skills and capacities required in the developmental phase transition to a different skill set. It is often desirable or necessary to bring in new leaders in the mature phase to replace those who were successful in the developmental phase.

REFERENCES

Entrepreneurs.com. 2002. "Business Plan Competitions." [Online article; retrieved 7/12/02.] http://entrepreneurs.about.com/cs/busplancontests/index.htm#m.

Forbes. 1998. "God Is His Business Planner." Forbes. [Online article; retrieved 7/29/02.] http://www.forbes.com/forbes/1998/0727/6202090a_print.html.

France, D. 1998. "Dr. Bernie Salick." New York Magazine July 20. [Online article; retrieved 8/6/02.] http://www.bentleyhealthcare.com/inthenews/newyork_0798.htm.

Rich, S. R., and D. E. Gumpert. 1985. "How to Write a Winning Business Plan." Harvard Business Review [May/June].

Sahlman, W. A. 1997. "How to Write a Business Plan." Harvard Business Review [July/August].

Chapter 5

Healthcare's Service-Line Management Revival

Outside healthcare, the past decade of consolidation in many industries and advances in market research and segmentation have created a boom in niche creation . . . We are seeing just the beginning of an explosion in niches brought on by an affluent, informed, demanding public and the plethora of information that is available to increasingly segment and subdivide in the pursuit of profitable niche markets.

—*Alan M. Zuckerman and Tracy K. Johnson (2001)*

REVIVING THE CENTERS-of-excellence strategy is much more than pouring old wine into new bottles. The healthcare market today is very different than the pre-managed care environment of the 1970s and early 1980s. With the rise of point-of-service and open-access health plans, consumers are regaining freedom of choice in the managed care market (Herrod 2001). Competition is intense. High-profile "super-doc" physicians are being recruited with six-figure financial incentives to add to their clinical reputations.

On the business side, MBA-trained service-line managers are brought in to coordinate brand strategy and operations. Internet-informed consumers will go coast-to-coast to participate in experimental clinical trials and get access to the top-ranked centers of excellence (COES). These specialized programs in services such as cardiology, cancer care, women's and children's services, orthopedics, rehabilitation, and neurosciences are the crème de la crème of the healthcare industry.

Focusing on clinical specialty care is not new. In the 1960s, President Lyndon Johnson appointed a presidential commission on heart disease, cancer, and strokes to address how the healthcare industry could improve treatment and outcomes (Walters 1999). One of the commission members, Houston's Dr. Michael DeBakey, proposed forming national networks of specialized medical centers of excellence. DeBakey's own Texas Heart Institute became a national model for high-volume cost efficiency with the best clinical outcomes. Today, the concept of centers of excellence may be the most popular strategy in the healthcare marketplace.

In a consumer-driven market, centers of excellence can be magnets for patient self-referral, physician recommendations, Internet channels, and top 100 or five-star ratings. Web-empowered consumers can easily find the best-of-the-best medical care.

Centers of excellence are also a business-to-business strategy. Hospitals may build volume and market share by engaging in carve-out contracting with managed care plans, third-party payers, self-insured employers, and the government. Medicare saved $41 million in seven pilot COE projects in the early 1990s and has attempted to expand direct contracting to more than 40 cardiovascular centers of excellence. More extensive COE contracting could be a future strategy to hold down Medicare spending. Dr. Arnold Milstein, medical director of the Pacific Business Group on Health, predicts that employers may offer bonuses to health plans that direct hospitals to high-volume specialty centers that earn top ratings for clinical outcomes and patient satisfaction (SMG Marketing Group 2001).

FOCUS, FOCUS, FOCUS

Centers of excellence are similar to Regina Herzlinger's concept of "focused factories" in her book *Market-Driven Healthcare: Who Wins, Who Loses in the Transformation of America's Largest Service Industry* (Herzlinger 1997). Dean Coddington, of McManis Consulting, and his colleagues predict that centers of excellence will be one of the basic characteristics of the health system of the future and warns that health systems that do not pursue a centers strategy may be vulnerable to competitors of all types who will fill the void (Coddington, Fisher, and Moore 2000).

Centers of excellence have a rich history, beginning a century ago with hospitals that specialized in particular customer segments, such as women, as well as procedures, such as joints and eye and ear surgery. Building and equipping centers of excellence was the most popular mode of clinical and business development for many hospitals in the 1970s and 1980s. But local competition and niche strategies were gradually supplanted by the trends of merger and integration in the mid- to late 1980s, when many regional markets were consolidated into two or three large systems. SMG Marketing Group (2001) reports that 331 integrated healthcare networks operated an average of seven specialized centers of excellence in 2000.

Returning to niche competition around centers of excellence is a practical solution for many system-affiliated hospitals now facing off with entrepreneurial, freestanding facilities owned by Wall Street–backed firms like HealthSouth and MedCath, as well as a new wave of competing ventures fostered by their own physicians in ambulatory surgery and imaging. Phil Newbold, FACHE, president and chief executive officer of Memorial Hospital and Health System in South Bend, Indiana, characterizes today's market as "not either-or, but kind of both-and," with a mix of back-to-basics approaches for some services and innovative new models for others (Haugh 2001).

Centers of excellence are not limited to large teaching hospitals with hundred-million-dollar capital budgets. They can be developed by hospitals of any size. In rural Pennsylvania, 102-bed Windber Medical Center has developed two centers of excellence—heart and cancer (Egger 2000). Windber is one of a dozen hospitals authorized to be a national Dr. Dean Ornish Heart Disease Reversal Program Center, under an innovative partnership with the Walter Reed Army Medical Center. Windber's new $7 million breast center is the second partnership with Walter Reed, which will provide research, medical informatics, risk management, clinical care, and a tissue bank. The small hospital's new breast care facility is designed using Planetree's patient-centered concepts. Located on a wooded site, it will provide an "almost womb-like" environment where patients can undergo testing and expect quick, confidential results, not the traditional two- to four-day anxiety-filled wait that many patients experience.

CLINICAL NICHE COMPETITION

Healthcare executives are worried that clinical niche competitors may take away their best business. Since the mid-1990s, niche players devoted to one medical condition or service have proliferated to fill gaps in the industry. Their key advantages over hospitals include their focus, entrepreneurial spirit, access to management expertise and Wall Street capital, and lack of baggage in partnering with physicians (Berry 1998). Legally, for-profit entrepreneurs can make deals with physicians that would be prohibited for tax-exempt organizations.

Niche competition is heating up rapidly, backed by venture capital and Wall Street investors, and hospitals and doctors are responding with new facilities of their own. Several entrepreneurial companies are active in the cancer field (see Table 5.1). Texas-based U.S. Oncology is the largest for-profit operator of outpatient cancer centers, with 76 cancer centers and 875 affiliated cancer specialists nationwide providing cancer care to over 15 percent of all newly diagnosed cancer patients annually (U.S. Oncology 2003).

In Philadelphia, the University of Pennsylvania offers one of the most comprehensive sets of clinical service lines in the United States. The university operates 11 multidisciplinary, specialty care centers supported by more than 1,000 physicians in 54 specialties (Health Care Advisory Board 1997a). More than 90 percent of its marketing and advertising budget is invested in the specialty service lines. Response from the public has been excellent. The specialty centers campaign has drawn 85,000 consumer calls resulting in 11,000 appointments and $4.6 million in new revenues. The University of Pennsylvania's specialty care service lines include a balance center, center for human appearance, smell and taste center, digestive and liver disorders center, cardiovascular center, cancer center, eye institute, neurological institute, musculoskeletal center, lung center, and skin laser center.

DEMOGRAPHIC NICHES

Healthcare marketers are targeting consumers by gender, age, and other demographic variables. Specialized health facilities are appearing across the nation, with programs oriented toward women, men, children, seniors, and other demographic segments.

Consumers who spend their own money on health services want and expect a perfect experience. Clinical and service processes are designed specifically for their target patients, with their expectations anticipated and met. Marketing guru Philip Kotler calls these processes "designed experiences" that control the environment and outcomes to enhance customer satisfaction (Kotler 1999). Customers are delighted to find health programs designed to cater to their needs in specialized facilities often separate from those shared by other patients. Designers of Stanford's Lucille Packard Children's Hospital crawled around on their knees to see a child's-eye view of mock-ups of the new units they were building. The results included a cut-down counter at pediatric nursing stations and child-high electric light switches in the patients' rooms. The Children's Hospital does share services with the University Medical Center at Stanford, but the transition to the adult facilities is seamless.

Table 5.1   **Growth of Outpatient Cancer Centers**

Year	Total Number of Cancer Centers	Percent Hospital Based
1997	600	N/A
1998	773	20%
1999	853	24%
2000	950	25%
2001	1,137	26%
2002	1,230	27%

Source: Verispan. 2003. *Outpatient Cancer Center Profiling Solution.* Newtown, PA: Verispan.

Fierce Demographic Competition

The competition is vigorous for these high-profile healthcare consumers. Companies like Pediatrix Medical Group, Inc., based in Fort Lauderdale, Florida, are creating national firms specializing in a customer segment. Pediatrix acquires pediatric practices and organizes them for managed care and clinical efficiency. Standardized clinical protocols and indicators drive quality across the practices. Centralized administrative services speed up billing, electronic claims, and collections. Networked computer systems link practices to share data, software, and medical research. Companies like Pediatrix can also manage multisite clinical trials for pharmaceutical manufacturers. Physician leadership and physician-led management are key to the success of these healthcare-niche-focused companies, argues David Hoskinson (1999), vice president of the medical group. Pediatrix believes that doctors managing doctors is an important differentiation from other physician practice management companies. A number of the company's top executives are physicians.

Customer Relationship Management

Database marketing is an increasingly popular method for encouraging repeat business (Kotler 1999). Also known as customer relationship management, this marketing methodology applied to healthcare combines consumer demographic information with disease-specific data. Although hospitals obviously must exercise great sensitivity in using patient information in their data warehouses for marketing purposes, the benefits are worthwhile. Examples of database marketing include the following:

- Reminders to women between 40 and 65 to schedule annual mammograms
- Follow-up marketing letter to postsurgical patients to have an orthopedic checkup at one or five years after their surgery
- Physician referral letter to emergency department patients suggesting they establish a regular relationship with a primary care physician from the hospital or medical group panel
- Annual birthday card and well-child checkup reminder for children born in the hospital

The payoffs for customer relationship management are repeat business and word-of-mouth reputation marketing. In the healthcare market, returning patients are often the best customers. Returning for more healthcare services after prior experiences demonstrates brand loyalty. Repeat customers may have many different reasons for returning, such as personal service, quality outcomes, price, convenience, insurance coverage, or familiarity with the provider's systems. Whereas new users are expensive—they need a lot of convincing, reports Sergio Zyman, former marketing vice president for Coca Cola—existing users "are efficient, they just need confirmation of their behavior and new reasons to buy your brand" (Zyman 1999).

SERVICE-LINE MANAGEMENT IS MARKET DRIVEN AND CUSTOMER CENTERED

The concept of service-line management is now more than a decade old in the health field, inspired by private industry's extensive use of product-line management by retail companies such as Proctor & Gamble and Johnson & Johnson. Renewed interest in service-line management is driven by the desire of many healthcare providers to increase revenues to offset reductions in Medicare payments due to the Balanced Budget Act. Niche-oriented strategies are revolutionizing healthcare, with entrepreneurial initiatives led by for-profit companies such as MedCath. In response, many hospitals and health systems are refocusing on their clinical centers of excellence, employing service-line management to coordinate ambulatory and postacute services across the continuum of care.

Today's efforts in service-line reorganization include a mix of financial, clinical, and market-share goals, including the following:

- Growing revenues through increased volume
- Providing a strong identity for key clinical services
- Taking excess costs permanently out of clinical processes
- Defining responsibility for clinical and financial performance
- Optimizing coordination of clinical care processes
- Integrating care in a patient-centered approach
- Increasing market share
- Creating recognized brand names
- Building customer loyalty and word-of-mouth referrals
- Improving customer service and satisfaction
- Providing excellent clinical outcomes and quality
- Competing in a report card environment

The fundamental principle of service-line management is organizing around the way patients receive services. Service-line management is different from traditional hospital department organization because it organizes services according to the way a patient receives care. It does not organize services according to function, available technology, or caregiver expertise. Functional departments such as lab, radiology, and surgery are criticized for acting like independent "silos," complains a service-line manager for cardiovascular and cardiorespiratory services at Allina Health System in Minneapolis, Minnesota (Anthony 1998). Too often, patients must be their own care coordinators across the many departments they rely on for services, with little cross-functional integration by the providers.

The goal of service-line management is to present an integrated continuum of services that is seamless and transparent to users. Service-line management creates sustainable advantages in cost efficiency and consumer preference by integrating clinical and business processes. Service lines are easy to access and use for both consumers and referring physicians. Patients' needs are anticipated. Administrative and clinical processes are put into place to move patients around the system as needed. Service delivery is efficient and responsive. In a service-line environment, patients are well informed and providers are experts in their specific tasks and roles.

The core of the service-line concept is organized clinical expertise. Physicians must be fundamentally involved in service-line management and marketing decisions, as well as clinical care, for the service-line concept to be fully operational. Hospitals that have introduced the service-line approach state they will not return to the traditional functional management approach (Health Care Advisory Board 1997a).

BUILDING REVENUES

Entrepreneurs target high-volume health services for one reason: cash flow. A steady stream of patients means a continuing revenue stream for the healthcare provider. The most popular high-volume services for a service-line approach include urgent care, ambulatory surgery, outpatient imaging and mammography, and laboratory testing. The challenge in high-volume niches is to provide prompt, efficient, and quality care to large numbers of patients, yet still meet consumer needs for personal service and privacy. Entrepreneurs have capitalized on high-volume facilities as attractive investment opportunities for physicians, despite federal Medicare regulations (Stark I, Stark II) that impose major restrictions on physician-owned health facilities.

A hospital emergency room can be a mini-mall of niche services such as emergency care, trauma care, chest-pain evaluation, psychiatric crisis, urgent care, pediatric walk-in clinic, and outpatient pharmacy. Baltimore, Maryland's Sinai Hospital recently opened an award-winning emergency department that featured seven distinct service offerings. The multiple-service concept is very appealing to patients who are segregated by service into more private facilities without the usual noise and confusion of a typical emergency department.

LOWERING THE COST STRUCTURE THROUGH SERVICE-LINE MANAGEMENT

Adopting a service-line approach can have a bottom-line effect on costs as well as revenues. Cost reduction is a direct result of reengineering focused very specifically on the core processes within the service line. Service-line managers are empowered to conduct a highly detailed examination of their service's direct and indirect costs, as well as fixed and variable costs. This analysis creates a platform of financial data for further cost analysis and benchmarking with peer programs. Cost-improvement initiatives can include clinical pathways, improved administrative processes, and intranet-enabled communications to speed up information flow.

In Houston, St. Luke's Episcopal Hospital has adopted a center-of-excellence approach that employs case management, outcomes management, and collaborative practice between physicians and nursing staff

(Anderson 1998). St. Luke's is home to the Texas Heart Institute, consistently ranked among the top ten cardiovascular centers in the United States.

Each service line at St. Luke's is a minibusiness, with its own management team, customers, marketing strategies, service integration strategies, budget, and bottom line. Service lines lend themselves to cost and quality-improvement strategies such as clinical pathways and disease management, where the care managers are located within the service-line organization. Every service line needs a critical mass of patients to be economically successful. The critical success factor for service lines, however, is decision-making authority over its budget (Anthony 1998). Hospital and health system administrators must be willing to delegate budget authority and bottom-line responsibility to service-line managers.

Cost-reduction targets of 10 percent are not unreasonable with a service-line management approach. In the Midwest, Community Hospitals Indianapolis (CHI) launched its service-line program in 1995, targeting the top 38 diagnosis-related groups and grouping them into 8 service lines that comprise over 50 percent of CHI's patient volume (Anthony 1998). CHI's service lines include behavioral care, cancer care, cardiovascular services, medical services, neurosciences, rehabilitation, and services for women and children.

Over a five-year period, the hospitals have achieved an overall cost reduction averaging 10 percent per adjusted discharge across the service lines. CHI set up multidisciplinary teams to create clinical pathways, with strong support from administration and physicians. When the service lines were formed, each was led by a physician and an executive director. Functions that crossed service lines, such as home care and health/wellness promotion, were grouped separately. Cost reductions have not affected quality. Patient satisfaction is high; some 91 percent of service-line patients at CHI rate their care as good, very good, or excellent.

CREATING NEW MARKET SPACE

Innovative healthcare marketers must stop competing head-to-head and focus on value innovation to create new market space for the service line. Too many companies have exactly the same view of the market, customers, and driving factors in the market. By thinking outside of the box, cutting-edge organizations can create new services and products that reinvent their industry. In healthcare, technology provides new service-line opportunities, such as minimally invasive surgery; marketing can accomplish similar opportunities, such as women's health centers. Repackaging services also creates new market space, such as combining services to create chest pain centers.

European strategy consultants W. Chan Kim and Renee Mauborgne (1999) outline a number of breakthrough techniques for marketing and service-line management (see Figure 5.1.) They recommend that strategists should consider the following:

- Substitute industries (e.g., health and vitamin stores)
- Strategic groups within industries (e.g., heart-only hospitals)
- Chains of buyers (e.g., direct employer-provider contracting for occupational health and medicine)
- Complementary product and service offerings (e.g., genetic testing lab services)
- Functional or emotional appeal to customers (e.g., cosmetic surgery and joint replacement)
- Time (e.g., services for the coming wave of seniors)

RESHAPING HEALTH INSURANCE USING SERVICE-LINE CONCEPTS

Service-line management is much more than a retail marketing concept. In a managed care marketplace, a service-line approach can respond to HMO and employer demands for bundling, package pricing, and specialty capitation. The most popular services for package pricing or subcapitation are mental health services, obstetrics, heart surgery, and occupational medicine. Management adviser George Longshore (1998) comments: "To compete in a managed care context, service-line management has to move beyond the clinical pathway model to a more financially oriented model—one that focuses not on treatment processes but on optimal price packaging, and not on marketing but on getting the best deal possible in managed care contracts."

When managed care plans say they are looking for "value" in shopping for service lines, they usually mean price. A service-line approach to the market allows an HMO to selectively contract with hospitals on a service-by-service basis. HMOs may be looking to contract with a high-reputation provider, such as cardiac surgery, or simply with a provider organization that offers the lowest price for a service package. Unbundling and bundling services has advantages to hospitals and medical groups, including "buying" volume with low-price packages or gaining access to a market-leading HMO through a subspeciality contract.

Figure 5.1   Shifting the Focus of Strategy

Competitive Factor	Traditional Strategy	New Strategic Focus
Core concept	Head-to-head competition	Creates new market space
Industry	Focuses on competitive position within strategic group	Looks across substitute industries
Strategic group	Focuses on rivals within its industry	Looks across strategic groups within its industry group
Buyer group	Focuses on better serving the buyer group	Redefines the buyer group of the industry
Scope of product and service offerings	Focuses on maximizing the value of product and service offerings within its industry	Looks across to complementary product and service offerings that go beyond the bounds of the industry
Functional-emotional orientation	Focuses on improving price-performance in line with functional-emotional orientation of its industry	Rethinks the functional-emotional orientation of its industry
Market shifts	Focuses on adapting to external trends as they occur	Participates in shaping external trends over time

Source: Kim, W. C., and R. Mauborgne. 1999. "Creating New Market Space." *Harvard Business Review* 77(1): 83–93.

Package pricing and specialty subcapitation contracting demand economic and clinical discipline by the provider. Risk means risk, and aggressive HMOs may set prices unrealistically low. Or the provider may not know its true costs of doing business and only learn the hard way what its costs are after agreeing to service-line pricing. Clinical pathways and disease-management programs are essential to financial success in service-line pricing arrangements. Providers also fear "de-capitation," where the health plan lowers the capitation rate or packaged price in years following the initial contract, forcing the provider to choose between losing volume or losing money. Because this "bait and switch" has happened frequently to California providers, physicians and hospitals in other regions are decidedly more cautious about capitation (Venable 1998).

SERVICE-LINE MANAGERS: A NEW BREED OF CLINICAL AND ADMINISTRATIVE MANAGERS

The SLM (service-line manager) is a new, multitalented healthcare executive. Service-line management requires a hybrid skill set that blends management tools with knowledge of the core clinical business. SLMs assemble and lead multidisciplinary teams. In healthcare organizations, the teams include physicians, nurses, care managers/discharge planners, therapists, and support personnel. A national survey of system-level marketing executives found a tremendous need for service-line administrators to ensure consistency in marketing and care management (Health Care Advisory Board 1998).

Communication is at the heart of service-line management. The process of integrating clinical care as well as marketing efforts relies on excellent communication skills and systems. Communication with physicians is one of the most important critical success factors for an SLM. In New Jersey, the AtlantiCare Health System has adopted a service-line approach. AtlantiCare's human resources vice president states: "A service line is only as successful as its manager's relations with the physicians who bring people in to use the service" (Longshore 1998). Physicians are the key ingredient in the multidisciplinary approach. Their support is essential and their objections must be addressed before service-line management can work.

Health organizations must learn from their private-sector competitors about building successful businesses in healthcare's niches. The SLM approach requires an entrepreneurial orientation combined with a clinical focus. The concept will work best if clinicians make both the business and patient care decisions. Service-line managers must have the appropriate business skills as well as clinical knowledge. The business world offers both risks and rewards. Service-line management thrusts hospitals and physicians into the market fray, putting them at risk for failure. Hospitals and health systems must take a page from the entrepreneur's playbook and put their service-line managers at risk for performance. To balance the risk, financial incentives and bonus opportunities must comprise at least 15 to 25 percent of compensation.

SEVEN STRATEGIES FOR SERVICE-LINE COMPETITION

Systemwide marketing and management are essential if the service-line approach is to succeed. Clinical services that target a particular population and provide well-defined services have the best potential to become recognized brands in their clinical niches. The following seven strategies provide a wide range of options for organizations that are pursuing the service-line-management approach.

1. Leveraging Brand-Name Reputation

For every Mayo Clinic and Johns Hopkins, dozens more superior hospitals and physician organizations offer brand-name status in their local markets and clinical service lines. To be a brand is to possess an established or invented reputation with consumers. A good brand represents trust. A brand name is only a symbol, but it can be a sustainable advantage in a competitive healthcare market. The average American is exposed to 3,000 commercial messages every day (Nilson 1998), and healthcare has now joined the marketing fray.

Branding is closely associated with another key marketing concept—positioning. According to Al Ries and Jack Trout (1981), authors of *Positioning: The Battle for Your Mind*, every product in consumers' minds is ranked on a "ladder" of preference. For each product category, consumers have a mental ladder that ranks the available options. The ranking is based on consumers' perception of value, which is a composite of quality, price, availability, and service.

In healthcare, rankings like those of *U.S. News & World Report* are based on physician ratings and medical referral patterns. According to a national survey sponsored by the Society for Healthcare Strategy and Market Development (1999) and the American Hospital Association, these rankings are expected to progressively influence consumers' choices and employers' selection of health plans.

2. Geographic Location

Location is a key reason for service-line success. Niche players typically target markets where the population is growing (at least 10 percent in five years), managed care has over 25 percent of the market, specialists' incomes are declining, and there are single-specialty medical groups of seven or more physicians (Berry 1998). Some organizations cluster their facilities to gain management and supply synergy as well as facilitate an exit from the market if the company decides to bundle and sell its facilities. Markets with low regulatory barriers to entry are popular with clinical niche entrepreneurs because it is faster and easier to establish new specialty care clinics in low-regulation markets like Texas that have eliminated certificates of need.

One of the keys to location is demographics—finding concentrations of target customers who fit the age, gender, and economic criteria. Niche medical practices and upscale service-line facilities are designed to attract insured patients and those with discretionary income. In Chevy Chase, Maryland, an affluent suburb of Washington, DC, internists have established the David Drew Clinic (2003), located in the penthouse suite of a high-rise building. The clinic was founded by a physician researcher at the National Institutes of Health who saw a niche for providing customized diagnostic testing not always covered by insurance.

Unlike this upscale approach, not all specialty care programs target the affluent. Many hospitals and health systems operate clinics specifically to serve low-income women, teens at high risk for pregnancy, seniors on Medicare and Medicaid, and the homeless, rather than to focus on profitability.

3. Physician Investment

The rising popularity of niche facilities and service lines is being accelerated by medical economics. Falling Medicare fees and health insurance fee schedules have tightened many physician's net incomes. Hospitals that will beat niche players at their own game will develop new economic partnerships with doctors to create focused clinical disciplines that are patient oriented. This approach will require sharing control with physicians and investing resources in facilities, technology, and infrastructure (Berry 1998).

Many of today's physicians and medical groups are looking for new revenue sources and new patient channels. Hospitals and doctors have engaged in a range of joint ventures since the 1970s, but state and federal rules have made these arrangements more difficult for tax-exempt healthcare providers in recent years. There are legal constraints on physician investment in service-line ventures. Federal regulations put strict limits on physician self-referral and ownership of health facilities. The Stark I and Stark II regulations can provide safe harbors for some physician economic joint ventures, including those engaged in integrated physician group practices. For-profit companies have more flexibility than tax-exempt hospitals. The regulations allow the proprietary companies to engage in economic arrangements that could put a nonprofit provider's tax status in jeopardy.

Local hospitals have competition for physician ventures. Doctors are responding positively to for-profit companies that both offer investment opportunities and give physicians more control over facilities and equipment in their clinical specialty. Hospitals in fear of a niche competitor should ask the question, "Do [our] physicians view [the hospital] as an attractive, trusted, long-term partner?" (Berry 1998). Community hospitals and health systems can be vulnerable to competition from a company with deep pockets that is willing to invest in the physicians' specialties and let the physicians share in the equity.

4. Comarketing/Cobranding

Bringing in a partner can boost the visibility and reputation of a service line. The partner organization can contribute its brand name, customer recognition, shared budget, and marketing expertise. Comarketing and cobranding prove especially helpful when launching a new service line. It also provides name recognition for a smaller facility or second-tier provider organization. World-class oncology center M.D. Anderson Cancer Center in Houston established a satellite oncology program within a community hospital in Orlando, Florida. The satellite increased access to oncology patients for the local hospital, raised the quality image of cancer care in the Orlando facility, increased market visibility for M.D. Anderson in the important Florida market, and brought in a referral flow of more complex patients to the Houston campus.

Other examples of marketing cooperation by colocation include the following (Bodel, Kowal, and Prince 1999):

- Mammography services located in an upscale department store
- Hospital-sponsored occupational health and wellness services in a local health club
- A satellite pediatric clinic in a suburban hospital 15 miles from its sponsor, an urban pediatric hospital

Colocation is another strategy for improving access to a service line. In Cleveland, Ohio, The Cleveland Clinic provided land for a new ambulatory care center for the Kaiser Health Plan, creating a win-win strategy for Kaiser and the clinic. The health plan enhanced its clinical reputation and market attractiveness by colocation on the clinic's campus, while the clinic built its primary care base and referrals for specialty care. This strategy offers new entry points into the system and expands the provider organization's feeder network for referrals. New strategic relationships can include both healthcare and nonhealth partners.

5. Outsourcing and Partnering

Outsourcing can be the better-faster-cheaper strategy for building or upgrading centers of excellence. On the business side, partners can bring a number of assets, including capital, specialized business systems, coding and billing expertise, interim or full-time management, strategic planning, marketing plans, advertising, staff recruitment and training, and customer satisfaction protocols. On the clinical side, the benefits of outsourcing can include an interim or full-time medical director, clinical pathways, clinical information systems, performance standards and benchmarks, nurse recruitment and staffing, physician recruitment and marketing, and top-name clinical consultants for periodic on-site services and off-site referrals.

The market reputation of the outsourcing partner can be a big plus for a new center of excellence or when the local organization wants to take its program to another level. Top hospitals and academic medical centers can lend their clinical prestige to raise the local image of clinical centers of excellence. Partners can accelerate the process of creating centers with off-balance-sheet financing, health facilities space plans, and construction management experience.

New centers of excellence are an expensive proposition that can be offset through partnering. Freestanding heart hospitals cost at least $40 million, and a comprehensive heart care ambulatory center requires at least $10 million (Jaklevic 2001). HealthSouth Corporation of Birmingham, Alabama, engages in both two-way (company and physicians) and three-way (company, physicians, and hospital) partnerships. With a management partner like HealthSouth, the company's expertise in businesses such as surgical centers and outpatient rehabilitation centers can shorten the learning curve and bring new centers to profitability in a shorter time frame.

6. E-Marketing

Marketing consultant Philip Kotler predicts that in the future, "marketing will be reengineered from A to Z in the 'Information Economy'" (Kotler 1999). Today more than 600 million people worldwide are connected to the Internet (CyberAtlas 2003). Business-to-consumer e-commerce reached $55.7 billion in 2001 and is expected to reach $113.2 billion in 2003, accounting for about 5 percent of total retail sales volume in the United States (Christopher 2003). Buyers and sellers can connect more conveniently, with information flowing across the nation, or around the globe, at virtually no cost. Time and distance will no longer be barriers to trade. The information revolution is all about consumer access; therefore, successful service lines must be easily accessible. Some of the most popular consumer access strategies include call centers, Internet access, web sites, and "push" technology that allows Internet users to have information sent automatically to their computers at regular intervals, such as news updates.

Net-enabled solutions will radically reduce the costs of today's marketing processes and create new cyber-channels for consumer interaction. Imagine the marketing possibilities for health organizations when the following information technologies are widely available:

- Computers, televisions, and telephones are linked to large-screen video entertainment centers for broadcasting healthcare infomercials.
- Intelligent systems operate a variety of systems remotely, such as in-home diagnostic monitoring equipment and automated drug-dispensing devices.
- Microvideo cameras are attached to computers for two-way video, backed by online data transmission and telephone communication for remote monitoring of chronically ill patients.
- Medical encyclopedias and online health advice are available on a 24-hour basis on the Internet.
- Voice-activated commands can control information systems, automated devices, and in-home equipment.
- Push technology regularly sends new clinical, product, and service information to the worried well and chronically ill.
- Patient support groups in chat rooms receive the latest medical information and online health advice.
- Call centers automatically route consumers through a health system and provide two-way patient monitoring and disease management for the homebound.
- Automated online order technology provides regular prompts to patients for renewal of prescription drugs and presents consumers

with health-oriented products for simultaneous ordering from healthcare cyber-pharmacies.

7. Cutting-Edge Technology

Implantation of the two-pound AbioCor artificial heart in several patients at Jewish Hospital in Louisville, Kentucky, has again put the spotlight on cardiology centers of excellence (Larson 2001). The plan for Jewish is simple: "We want to be in the same league with the Johns Hopkins and the Mayos," declares Doug Shaw, FACHE, president (Romano 2001). The centers-of-excellence strategy has been 25 years in the making for Jewish, which made a strategic decision in the 1990s to concentrate on a few clinical specialties such as hand surgery and cardiac care and transplantation. Jewish has invested $8.2 million in the artificial heart project, while AbioCor research and development costs exceed $60 million. AbioCor pumps will now be implanted at other heart centers, including the Texas Heart Institute in Houston, University of California Los Angeles, Hahnemann University Hospital in Philadelphia, and Massachusetts General Hospital in Boston.

Many other centers of excellence have built their reputations on high-tech platforms. In cancer care, therapeutic advances include new combinations of pharmaceuticals, radiation, and chemotherapy. Radiation therapy has evolved considerably since linear accelerators were first introduced in the 1950s (Becker 2001). They have gone from analog to digital, and multileaf collimators were added in the 1990s to significantly improve the precision of radiation therapy. Doctors can now sculpt the radiation beams using automated three-dimensional conformal radiation therapy. Even newer technology, intensity-modulated radiation therapy, allows radiologists to attack tumors with a pencil-thin beam that spares healthy tissue. Higher radiation doses that deliver greater precision improve outcomes. New York's Memorial Sloan-Kettering Cancer Center reports that 90 percent of patients treated with megadoses of radiation were cancer free after three years, versus only 40 percent of those treated with the lowest radiation dose.

CHALLENGES OF IMPLEMENTATION

Not every clinical service lends itself to the service-line approach. If no well-defined target population or constellation of services exists, the service-line concept may not fit. Staff and services often overlap between service lines, causing marketing issues, as well as making it difficult to maintain consistent processes for managing patients within the clinical service niche. In a national survey, the Health Care Advisory Board found that behavioral health, neurology, and orthopedic service lines were not common among typical health systems because of the degree of difficulty associated with extending a service-line approach across the multiple facilities and service providers (Health Care Advisory Board 1998).

Implementing and maintaining a service-line approach in a health organization poses a number of challenges to success. These challenges include the following (Health Care Advisory Board 1997a):

- Managing across functional and service departments
- Mediating turf issues, lack of trust, and interorganizational rivalry
- Managing higher communications demands
- Addressing lack of management authority and fiscal control by service-line managers
- Implementing a matrix-model management reporting structure (e.g., nursing, operations, and finance)
- Establishing common leadership across the service lines
- Maintaining consistent processes across multiple sites
- Implementing centralization of service-line management versus decentralization of care
- Teaching service-line managers to perform strategic business planning
- Gaining physician acceptance and support
- Developing new financial systems and reports
- Determining labor distribution and allocating costs
- Analyzing clinical outcomes
- Coordinating information systems
- Developing a unified marketing strategy
- Promising (but not delivering) improved patient satisfaction

CONCLUSION

Only a few years ago, marketing gurus were in vogue among U.S. hospitals and health systems. Many healthcare provider organizations spent millions on advertising and marketing, despite the fact that healthcare is an intangible product that is difficult to brand or market. Advertising spending by healthcare providers has had mixed results. In a number of hospitals and health systems, the experiment with marketing and service lines lasted only three to five years.

By the early 1990s, managed care was becoming dominant in many markets. It rapidly became obvious that patients were being steered to hospitals and physicians based on their HMO contracts. Providers' management focus shifted into managed care contracting and away from marketing. Under these market conditions, service-line management and marketing often melted away.

Today's resurgent interest in service-line management could be just another fad. The healthcare industry is quick to adopt new management ideas from the private sector—and often just as quick to drop them. Market-oriented provider organizations across the nation have learned a number of lessons about service-line management in the decade since the concept was introduced.

- Physician involvement is critical for success in creating and managing clinical service lines.
- Service-line revenue and cost accounting is necessary to manage the business and evaluate bottom-line results.
- Service-line managers need a clinical background to understand their core business as well as business training to manage and market their service.
- Market research on customer needs and expectations provides an essential baseline for conducting marketing and advertising campaigns.
- Service-line management requires a multidisciplinary approach involving physicians, nurses, therapists, administrative management, and marketing staff.
- Service-line managers must own their businesses and have real control over their budgets.
- Each service line exists in its unique minimarket of competitors and substitutes, often including some competition within the provider organization.
- Creating new brand names is a costly and time-consuming process that can confuse customers if not done well in a sustained marketing effort.
- Corporate overhead can kill a potentially successful service line by increasing fixed costs without adding value.

Service-line management can inspire a clash of corporate cultures between clinical caregivers and administrators. The whole business lexicon is disturbing to some health professionals, who sometimes feel that finances can be more important than patients. Even if they show an interest, many clinical department heads and physician chiefs of services have only limited management training. They may be superb clinicians, but not all have the entrepreneurial spirit or business management tools to become successful service-line managers. One-day seminars on developing business plans will not produce MBA types who can develop detailed financial pro formas.

Healthcare professionals are still skeptical about adopting business strategies and infusing them into health organizations. A Pennsylvania physician is openly critical about the business orientation of most hospitals: "In essence, administrators run hospitals like a Burger King. Hospital administrators want patients to be happy so they will come back and bring their insurance money with them" (Crippen 1998). Business-minded administrators must ensure that their service-line strategies put patients first and respond to community needs as well as the provider organization's need for additional revenues.

REFERENCES

Anderson, J. 1998. "Creating a Center of Excellence." *Radiology Management* 20 (2): 23–29.

Anthony, S. J. 1998. "Two Approaches to Service-Line Management: Community Hospitals Indianapolis and Rural Maine's York Hospital." *Strategic Healthcare Excellence* 11 (4): 1–9.

Becker, L. 2001. "Therapy on Target: Change in Reimbursement Helps Advance a New Radiation Technology." *Modern Healthcare* 31 (24): 34, 38.

Berry, K. 1998. "Niche Players: Your Next Challenge." *Trustee* 5 (7): 27–28.

Bodel, D. R., S. F. Kowal, and J. M. Prince. 1999. "Second Wave Relationships: The Quest for Revenue." *Health Forum Journal* 42 (1): 42–45.

Christopher, G. 2003. "Online Sales Still Fastest Growing Segment of Total Retail Sales." [Online article; retrieved 8/1/03.] www.christopher-inc.net/articles/tdmv5n7.htm.

Coddington, D., E. A. Fisher, and K. D. Moore. 2000. "Characteristics of Successful Health Care Systems." *Health Forum Journal* 43 (6): 40–45.

Crippen, D. M. 1998. "What's Wrong with Treating Medicine Like a Business?" *Cost & Quality* 4 (4): 19–20.

CyberAtlas. 2003. "Global Online Populations." [Online information; retrieved 8/5/03.] http://cyberatlas.internet.com/big_picture/geographics/article/0,1323,5911_151151,00.html.

David Drew Clinic. 2003. "Unique Approaches." [Online article; retrieved 8/5/03.] http://www.daviddrew.com/frame.html.

Egger, E. 2000. "Tiny Hospital Continues to Pursue New Initiatives, Launches Breast Center." *Health Care Strategic Management* 18 (8): 13–14.

Haugh, R. 2001. "Hospitals Rethink Their Integration Strategies. Back to Basics." *Hospitals & Health Networks* 75 (1): 33–35.

Health Care Advisory Board. 1997a. "Product-Line Management at the Executive Level." *Fact Brief* (June): 1–9.

———. 1997b. *Future Revenues: Sources of Sustainable Revenues for America's Health Systems.* Special Report. Washington, DC: Health Care Advisory Board.

——— 1998. "System-Wide Product-Line Development." *Issue Brief* (December): 1–25.

Herrod, K. G. 2001. "Marketing and Branding Your Centers of Excellence." *Managed Care Quarterly* 9 (2): 50–54.

Herzlinger, R. 1997. *Market-Driven Healthcare: Who Wins, Who Loses in the Transformation of America's Largest Service Industry.* Cambridge, MA: Harvard Business School Press.

Hoskinson, D. 1999. Pediatrix Medical Group, Fort Lauderdale, FL. Author communication, May 20.

Jaklevic, M. C. 2001. "A Deal That's Hard to Refuse." *Modern Healthcare* 31 (49): 4–5, 9.

Kim, W. C., and R. Mauborgne. 1999. "Creating New Market Space." *Harvard Business Review* 77 (1): 83–93.

Kotler, P. 1999. *Kotler on Marketing: How to Create, Win and Dominate Markets.* New York: Free Press.

Larson, L. 2001. "Deciding to Pioneer: What Does It Take?" *Trustee* (July 21). [Online article; retrieved 11/11/02.] http://www.trusteemag.com.

Longshore, G. 1998. "Service-Line Management/Bottom-Line Management." *Journal of Health Care Finance* 24 (4): 72–79.

Nilson, T. H. 1998. *Competitive Branding: Winning in the Market Place with Value-Added Brands.* New York: John Wiley & Sons.

Ries, A., and J. Trout. 1981. *Positioning: The Battle for Your Mind.* New York: Warner Books.

Romano, M. 2001. "That Giant Whirring Sound You Hear." *Modern Healthcare* 31 (37): 28–33.

SMG Marketing Group. 2001. "2001 Guide to Healthcare Market Segments." Chicago: SMG Solutions.

Society for Healthcare Strategy and Market Development. 1999. "Beyond 2000: Health Trends in the New Millennium." Chicago: American Hospital Association, 1–24.

U.S. Oncology. 2003. "Company Overview." [Online information; retrieved 8/2/03.] http://www.usoncology.com/CompanyInfo/default.asp.

Venable, R. S. 1998. *Capitation: Tools, Trends, Traps and Techniques.* Los Angeles: Practice Management Information Company.

Verispan. 2003. *Outpatient Cancer Center Profiling Solution.* Newtown, PA: Verispan.

Walters, P. D. 1999. "Centers of Excellence: Historic Trends and Future Decisions." *Journal of Cardiovascular Management* 10 (4): 17–24.

Zuckerman, A. M., and T. K. Johnson. 2001. "Returning to Revenue Growth." Part 1. *Health Progress* 82 (2): 19–21, 79.

Zyman, S. 1999. *The End of Marketing As We Know It.* New York: HarperBusiness.

Chapter 6

From Reducing Medical Errors to Real Quality Improvement

Even as the debate goes on [in Congress], providers are moving forward quietly to try to improve their medical errors rate, and physicians and physician executives are in the forefront of attempts to change the process of care delivery—and with it, the underlying culture of know-nothingism that has long pervaded American medicine.

Mark Hagland (2000)

HOSPITALS AND PHYSICIANS were shocked when the Institute of Medicine (IOM) released its blockbuster report in November 1999 that estimated between 44,000 and 98,000 patients die each year because of medical errors in hospitals across the United States. The report was a devastating critique of American medicine, exposing a pattern of miscommunication and medical blunders even in hospitals where care was thought to be the gold standard (Kohn, Corrigan, and Donaldson 2000). The estimate of up to 98,000 deaths annually is more than breast cancer, highway accidents, or AIDS, according to the 223-page report. The federal government endorsed the IOM's goal of reducing errors 50 percent within five years through a combination of research and reporting. In a follow-up report, *Crossing the Quality Chasm,* the IOM called for a national program of errors reduction, including funding of $30 to $35 million per year for the creation of a federal Center for Patient Safety within the Agency for Healthcare Research and Quality (AHRQ), as well as grants to develop and install technology for medical-error reporting in all U.S. hospitals (IOM 2001).

Improving the quality of American medical care is a powerful trend, reflecting the growing influence of consumerism. A study by Arthur Andersen and the Health Forum, the San Francisco–based division of the American Hospital Association, focused on consumer expectations of the highest quality as one of the key drivers of twenty-first-century healthcare (Geniat and Johnson 2000). Quality, as defined by consumers, includes not only the absence of medical errors but also the patients' interactions with physicians, support staff, and technology and how the system deals with people. But will the health system respond? The Andersen study found that healthcare leaders were conflicted about customers versus costs.

THE HIGH COST OF ERRORS

According to studies by Superior Consultant, a healthcare information management consulting firm, medication errors cost an estimated $2,500 to $3,500 per bed per year (Zaffrin 2000). Such costs could add up to $1.6 million yearly for a 450-bed hospital. In one pilot study, a large teaching hospital spent $5 million dealing with adverse drug reactions. Where do drug errors take place? A study conducted by the Food and Drug Administration in 2001 revealed that 42 percent of the medication errors were attributable to human errors, such as knowledge or performance deficits, miscalculation of dosage or infusion rates, drug preparation or transcription errors, fatigue, and computer errors. Labeling problems accounted for 20 percent of the medication errors, while communication (19 percent), name confusion (13 percent), and packaging design (6 percent) were the causes of the remaining errors (FDA 2001).

Despite significant capital investments by hospitals in information technology and electronic medical records, quality management experts cite an analytic gap as a major reason that clinical care is not better managed and patterns of medical errors are missed (Brailer et al. 1996).

In Philadelphia, CareScience has partnered with the University of Pennsylvania to develop CaduCIS (Clinical and Administrative Decision-Support Utility and Clinical Information System), a care management software package. In a pilot project with the Graduate Health System, care managers identified an unexpectedly high rate of complications in patients with congestive heart failure (CHF). Automating the data analysis reduced the amount of time by a factor of 10:1 that doctors would have spent in chart review to identify the causes of the complications. Care managers also identified one widely used test in CHF management that had no apparent clinical benefit, saving $8 per test for 3,000 patients per year. The project demonstrates that clinical performance improvement pays off in lower complication rates and associated costs, less use of expensive tests and therapies, and more efficient staff time in problem analysis and improving clinical pathways.

IS THE NATION'S HEALTH THREATENED BY MEDICAL ERRORS?

If the IOM study is accurate, the unintended errors of modern hospital care are equivalent to one 747 aircraft crash every day. In the wake of the study, the venerable Institute of Medicine found itself in the middle of a raging debate over the adequacy of the data and the validity of the scientific analyses behind its error study. In the *Journal of the American Medical Association*, critics shot back with an article entitled "Deaths Due to Medical Errors Are Exaggerated in Institute of Medicine Report" (McDonald, Weiner, and Hui 2000). They argue that today's hospitalized patients have "high disease burdens and high death risks," suggesting that most in-hospital deaths will occur regardless of how many "accidents" are avoided. In a similar article in the *New England Journal of Medicine*, a physician from Boston-based Brigham and Womens Hospital cautions that "careful readers must have some reservations" about the IOM report (Brennan 2000).

The Institute of Medicine report has outraged consumer organizations and health insurers, who are calling for new federal legislation to require mandatory reporting of medical mishaps. Congressional proposals have centered on a no-fault system like that used by pilots to report safety lapses and in-air near misses. The American Hospital Association and American Medical Association have been highly vocal in their rejection of mandatory reporting and increased federal oversight. They fear that reporting will be mandatory and that error data will be public, exposing hospitals and physicians to a flurry of lawsuits.

A federal bureaucracy is already being established that could provide oversight for a national program in medical errors. The Agency for Healthcare Research and Quality has the congressional mandate to provide leadership in error reporting and process improvement. The agency spent much of the 1990s developing medical practice guidelines, but heavy opposition from the American Medical Association and other medical groups curbed the federal initiatives for defining national standards of practice.

DARTMOUTH ATLAS RAISES QUESTIONS ABOUT PRACTICE VARIATIONS

Variation in clinical practice is a national challenge for healthcare providers and purchasers. The *Dartmouth Atlas of Health Care*, developed by the Center for Evaluative Clinical Sciences of the Dartmouth Medical School, has made a science of the geography of healthcare in the United States (Dartmouth Medical School 2000). In collaboration with the

American Hospital Association, researchers at Dartmouth are committed to establishing a new model of clinical decision making that applies benchmarks of performance. The *Atlas* was written by a remarkable father-son team, John Wennberg, M.D., director of Dartmouth Medical School's Center for Evaluative Health Sciences, and son David Wennberg, M.D., director of the Center for Outcomes Research and Evaluation at the Maine Medical Center.

For a variety of major conditions, the *Dartmouth Atlas* is vivid proof that dozens of local medical markets experience 30 percent higher use rates than the national average, while many other regions are lower than national benchmarks. The *Atlas* relies on a 20 percent sample of Medicare patients, based on a national small-area analysis of 313 hospital referral regions.

According to the *Dartmouth Atlas,* costs of care in the last six months of life vary tremendously. Use of intensive care in the last six months varies for no apparent medical or demographic reason. In Newark, New Jersey, some 41.5 percent of dying patients were cared for in an intensive care unit (ICU), as were 47.5 percent of patients in Miami, Florida—but only 26.8 percent of terminal patients in Milwaukee, Wisconsin, and 25 percent in Seattle, Washington, were given the costly treatment of intensive care.

Researchers at Dartmouth find in many local markets that variations in clinical practice are more common than similarities. In Louisiana, the referral rate for radical prostatectomies in Baton Rouge is 4.9 procedures per 1,000 population, the highest in the nation; in nearby Lafayette, the rate is 0.9 per 1,000, the lowest. In terms of medical procedures, data from the *Dartmouth Atlas* suggest that geography is destiny, according to Dr. Jack Lord, former chief operating officer for the American Hospital Association, which publishes the atlas (Moore 1998).

The *Dartmouth Atlas* also demonstrates that the more hospital beds are in the local market, the higher the use rates and health costs are likely to be. Louisiana, where the hospital bed–to-patient ratio is in the highest quintile, is also one of the highest-cost states, where an above-average number of Medicare patients die in hospitals. These large swings in use rates and health costs found in the *Dartmouth Atlas* suggest wasted resources and opportunities for clinical cost management for every hospital and health system in America.

QUALITY IS A BUSINESS STRATEGY

The payoffs from clinical quality improvement could be millions of dollars of eliminated rework, savings that could put every hospital in

America in the black. The Institute of Medicine estimates that the cost of nonfatal medical errors is $17 to $19 billion each year (Rovner 2000). According to the IOM, between 2.9 and 3.7 percent of all hospital admissions had an injury from medical management (Benjamin 2000).

"Quality is a business strategy," at the Sacred Heart Medical Center in Spokane, Washington (Davis 2000). The hospital set a three-year, $10 million target for cost reduction by lowering the incidence of medical errors. Working with Bridge Medical Inc., which provides error reporting software, Sacred Heart has found that 10 to 15 percent of its operating costs involve duplicative rework and complications caused by adverse events, as much as $40 to $50 million. Bridge Medical estimates a savings of over $1.6 million at the hospital annually by addressing the problem of medication errors. At a cost of $95 per preventable error and an error rate of 1 percent, Sacred Heart can significantly lower its costs per discharge with research and development and information systems investment of less than $500,000. Sacred Heart's chief executive officer also reports nursing productivity gains of 20 minutes per registered nurse per shift, and the hospital's malpractice insurance costs have been reduced by the carrier by 10 percent.

Providers can learn from other industries about competing on quality. Gary Mecklenburg, CHE, chief executive officer of Northwestern Memorial Hospital in Chicago, argues that hospitals and health systems must overcome their isolation from other industries and learn from the private sector: "Today, healthcare organizations are subject to the same economic forces, the same business principles, and the same standards that exist for the rest of the economy" (Lanser 2000).

The efforts by a number of provider organizations to systematically reduce medication errors—perhaps the most frequent source of medical mistakes—are promising. The Veterans Administration (VA) has installed electronic monitoring systems for medication administration in nearly one of four VA facilities. At the VA pilot site in Topeka, Kansas, the Colmery-O'Neil VA Medical Center experienced a 64 percent reduction in medical errors in comparison with its baseline error rates from 1993, the last year the VA relied on a fully paper-based medication administration system (IHC 2000). In fact, these dramatic results may even be understated; VA officials believe that error rates in the past were probably underreported because they relied on people reporting their own mistakes.

PROVIDERS TACKLE THE ISSUES OF REDUCING ERRORS AND VARIATION

Providers are striking back at the criticism of their quality with publicity and process improvement. The National Coalition on Health Care and the Institute for Healthcare Improvement produced a report, *Reducing Medical Errors and Improving Patient Safety: Success Stories from the Front Lines of Medicine* (NCHC and IHF 2000). At St. Louis–based SSM Health Care, Dr. Andrew Kosseff, an internist, has taken the lead in a year-long clinical collaborative project inspired by the Institute for Healthcare Improvement. Led by Dr. Donald Berwick, the institute has pioneered quality improvement efforts for 20 years. SSM's initiative covers 21 hospitals in four states. Three projects are currently underway, including evaluating prescribing practices, secondary prevention of ischemic heart disease, and using patient information to improve healthcare delivery.

In Salt Lake City, Intermountain Health Care has relentlessly pursued a program of clinical process improvement for more than a decade. Dr. Brent James, vice president for medical research, reports a 75 percent improvement in drug errors and quality problems at the system's flagship LDS Hospital (Hagland 2000). Problems such as patient falls, nosocomial infections, decubitus ulcers, blood transfusion errors, and pulmonary embolisms arising from deep vein thrombosis have been targets for clinical process management.

Further improvements in quality are possible. When Intermountain applied intensive computer analysis to drug errors at LDS Hospital, it found 80 times more adverse drug events, but few hospitals have the databases and tools to match this performance.

Hospitals are adding quality indicators to their "dashboard" reports of key benchmarks of organizational performance. At a recent conference for strategic planners and marketing executives sponsored by Rand Healthcare Roundtables, several provider initiatives in constructing management dashboards were profiled.

At the St. Luke's Hospitals in Boise, Idaho, the board of directors took the lead in asking management to give them a snapshot of the business in a continuing report series (O'Keeffe 2000). The 14-factor report includes such quality indicators as emergency department treatment times, patient satisfaction, perioperative deaths, and unscheduled readmissions.

Community Health Care, a regional health system in central Wisconsin, has used dashboard indicators for five years (Day 2000). Its report was inspired by the Juran Institute and is issued monthly on critical performance measures. Thirteen indicators provide the board and management with continuous updates on growth, performance, and service and quality, including patient occurrences per 1,000 days; number of customer complaints; patient satisfaction; and readmissions within three days per 1,000 discharges.

MEDICATIONS MANAGEMENT
Medication errors, adverse drug events, and what the Joint Commission on Accreditation of Healthcare Organizations (Joint Commission) refers to as sentinel events cost each healthcare system as much as one million dollars annually (Classon et al. 1997). A medical mistake is considered "an unintended act with potentially negative consequences for the patient, which would be judged wrong by skilled and knowledgeable peers, independent of whether the patient was actually harmed" (Classon et al. 1997).

The implementation of a medication management solution with built-in quality checks will help organizations reduce their incidence of medical mistakes—specifically medication errors—while reducing associated costs with managing medication inventory. Preventable adverse drug events occur at four stages (Bates et al. 1995):

1. *Ordering by physician (56 percent of medication errors)*: Wrong dose, wrong choice of drug, patient has a known allergy to the drug.
2. *Administration of medication orders by nursing staff (34 percent of medication errors)*: Wrong drug, wrong dose of drug administered, wrong time (drug not sent in time to be given to patient at time ordered), wrong technique used to administer drug.
3. *Transcribing of medication order by secretarial staff (6 percent of medication errors)*: Wrong frequency of drug administration, missed dose because medication is not transcribed.
4. *Dispensing of medications ordered by the pharmacy department (4 percent of medication errors)*: Wrong time, wrong drug, wrong dose.

The medication management process in hospitals has not evolved to the same degree technologically as other clinical processes. Today's processes rely heavily on oral or written communication of various clinicians and administrative personnel across various functions within the hospital. The medication management process affects registrars, physicians, nurses, pharmacists, finance, quality/risk management, materials management, and the patient, with many activities taking place far from the bedside.

A process of this complexity poses significant opportunities for error. The medication management process begins at the time the patient is admitted or enters the organization and includes processes associated with medication ordering, transcription, and dispensing; continues with the administering and documenting of medications given to patients; and includes posting charges, updating inventory, and replenishing stock. Quality- and/or risk-management processes are affected retrospectively when errors occur.

In a pilot project in a North Carolina medical center, point-of-care systems for positive bar code identification resulted in significant improvements in medications processes, including a 52 percent reduction in doses omitted, a 43 percent decrease in medications delivered at the wrong time, and a 33 percent drop in the wrong drugs being administered (Zaffrin 2000).

Medication management solutions in their ultimate implementation address all the components of the process: ordering, clinical checking, drug distribution, automated drug dispensing device (e.g., PYXIS) interfaces, point-of-care positive patient/drug identification via bar code, documentation of medication administration, charge capture based on administration, supply chain management, and error and outcomes analysis.

Studies have shown that about 35 percent of all medication errors occur at the point of administration, which until recently was not easy to automate, track, or quality assure. Advancements in radio-frequency networks and mobile computing capabilities are making point-of-care devices and bar code technology more acceptable to the healthcare industry. This technology now makes it possible to verify the right drug, for the right patient, prior to administration, at the point of care. The combination of high-tech devices and the ability to eliminate serious medication errors has become the highlight feature of medication management offerings. While technology alone is not a medication management solution, it has become the focus of many vendors who seek to integrate technology into their existing medication management components.

CLINICAL INFORMATION TECHNOLOGY

Computerization of the clinical care process is gaining momentum. Spurred by the message in the Institute of Medicine reports, hospitals are boosting their investments in clinical information technology. An industry survey by McKinsey & Company projected that hospital spending on information technology would rise 6 to 7 percent per year through 2004, but that clinical information technology expenditures would grow strongly at rates of 13 to 15 percent annually in this period (Morrisey 2001). Another study of healthcare information technology spending by research firm Gartner, Inc., reported that more than 50 percent of responding healthcare executives planned to add a clinical decision-support system to their healthcare information system in the next two years (Morrisey 2001). Administrators are realizing that clinical care management is the final frontier in operational improvement. Consultants caution that hospitals seeking to improve clinical performance should put their priority on health outcomes, but that cost reduction will be a natural side benefit.

The nation's high-tech hospitals are demonstrating the benefits of clinical information technology investments. According to the American Hospital Association's annual survey, the "most wired" hospitals improved paid hours per adjusted discharge by 3.8 percent, while all other hospitals only improved productivity by 1.8 percent (Solovy 2001). This improvement allowed the most-wired hospitals to earn significantly more operating income per staff member over other facilities, with information technology playing a critical role in streamlining operations.

Employers believe such systems can lead to a reduction of medical errors by as much as 85 percent, by eliminating mistakes in transcription of written orders. Hospitals are hearing the employers' message. The Gartner organization reported that 60 percent of hospitals planned to add a physician order-entry system in 2002 to 2003 (Morrisey 2001).

Consulting firms and technology manufacturers are expanding their offerings and technical support in clinical information technology systems. McKesson Information Solutions, the nation's largest vendor of information technology with more than 1,000 hospital clients, recently purchased a physician-oriented clinical information technology system from Vanderbilt University for $20 million. Rival Siemens Medical Solutions Health Services Corporation, formerly Shared Medical Systems, is also investing in a new set of applications designed to reduce inefficiency in clinical processes. Cerner Corporation is experiencing very rapid growth due to the popularity of the company's clinical information systems. GE Medical Systems is also experiencing strong sales. McKinsey consultant Mikael Ohman cautions, however, that today's rapid growth of clinical information solutions "must be matched by performance that meets expectations" or hospital spending will slow (Morrisey 2001).

WHY QUALITY IMPROVEMENT EFFORTS FAIL

Many hospitals and health systems have initiated quality improvement, but often with mixed results. David Shulkin, M.D., identifies a number of failings that can reduce the effectiveness of quality initiatives: too many meetings, overemphasis on process, need for incentives, organizational and personality barriers, too much data, reliance on outside benchmarks, no accountability for results, too long a time line, too many quality improvement projects, and not knowing when to call it quits (Shulkin 2000).

Underinvestment in information technology is another limiting factor. Mark Leavitt, chairman of Medscape, complains that healthcare organizations spend only 3.9 percent of their budgets on information technology, in comparison with banking, which spends more than 10 percent and has automated many routine processes (Tedeschi 2000).

Medicare budget cuts and managed care have slashed many hospitals' capital budgets, deferring investment in upgrades. In Worcester, the University of Massachusetts Medical Center has invested more than $40 million in information technology over the past five years but is a long way from putting Palm-type electronic medical records in the hands of its physicians. The information system does not have enough capacity for x-rays and digital images to be sent across the hospital's network. Only the intensive care unit and emergency department have that capability. "We lose money on every admission," notes a University of Massachusetts senior executive. The hospital will focus on technology upgrades, but it cannot afford Windows 2000. This situation is far from the vision of e-health that drives the hospital's information technology managers, but it is the reality until more capital becomes available (Tedeschi 2000).

SEVEN STEPS TOWARD MORE EFFICIENT CARE

Placing a high management priority on clinical improvement is much more than reducing medical errors. There is a synergy among quality improvement, disease management, clinical efficiency, and patient satisfaction. At Lovelace Health Systems in Albuquerque, New Mexico, a disease management program for clinical depression saved one million dollars (Reeder 2000). A similar program is underway at Sharp HealthCare, with a goal to improve the underdiagnosis of depression in patients who are presenting to the health system for a variety of other ailments, such as chest pain and back pain.

Following are seven successful strategies for reducing medical errors and improving clinical performance.

1. Science of Error Management

What is needed is a new science of errors that tracks deviations from standards and benchmarks and probes lapses of care, such as nosocomial infections, patient falls, and medication errors (Weber 2000a). Systematic progress in the science of errors requires the following three ingredients:

1. A no-fault error-reporting system that records a high percentage of all errors
2. Extensive computerized databases of clinical performance with information-technology-facilitated data analysis
3. A management process for disseminating information and improving clinical performance

Hospitals should develop a voluntary reporting system of medical errors in the short term. Hospital and health system administrators are advised to find out how large a problem the organization may have now, develop an error-reduction plan, and prepare for the likelihood of mandatory reporting, which could be imposed by the government within the next two to three years. States may not wait for Washington to enact their own errors oversight legislation. The state of Massachusetts has created a coalition to examine ways to prevent medical errors, and Maryland's Health Care Commission has also begun to investigate this issue.

In Michigan, the Borgess Medical Center of Kalamazoo was dismayed to discover a much higher than expected mortality rate for nonsurgical heart cases (CareScience 2000). According to data published annually by the Michigan Hospital Association, the hospital's mortality data were above expected benchmark levels. Although cardiology is a major service line for Borgess, which is nationally recognized as one of the top 100 hospitals for interventional cardiology, the nonsurgical mortality experience for a group of 15 DRGs and 1,500 patients was unexpectedly high. The hospital brought in CaduCIS and the Institute for Management Development, a division of CareScience.

Three DRGs for management of acute myocardial infarction (AMI) were found to account for the greatest deviation from risk-adjusted predicted mortality. The researchers recommended a number of actions, including targeting noncardiologists for continuing medical education in the latest treatment protocols. In the three-month period following the implementation of improvement strategies for AMI patients, the mortality rate decreased from 19 percent to 8 percent.

2. Electronic Medical Records

The electronic medical record is much more than an automated paper record—it is a database and decision-support system. In California's trendsetting San Diego market, Sharp HealthCare believes that investing in electronic medical records is a fundamental key to gaining efficiency and restoring financial profitability. Taking the waste out of clinical processes can generate significant return on investment for Sharp's four general acute hospitals, three specialty facilities, and three large affiliated medical groups (Reeder 2000). John Byrnes, M.D., Sharp's senior vice president for clinical effectiveness, was formerly responsible for the extensive clinical engineering and benchmarking program at Albuquerque's Lovelace Clinic. He is now overseeing the installation of an electronic medical records system at Sharp. In the intensively competitive San Diego market, with one of the highest managed care penetration rates in the nation, Byrnes believes that it is "absolutely imperative that in addition to delivering quality care, that we be able to prove that we can deliver quality care" (Reeder 2000).

Collecting data about the frequency, nature, and severity of errors is essential to create a baseline, record deviations from standards and procedures, and analyze performance over time.

3. Patient-Centered Clinical Improvement

Clinical improvement programs should be designed around patients, not providers. The baseline for successful disease management programs is patient-centered care, believes Byrnes (Reeder 2000). In the Lovelace experience, when clinical performance improvement programs are designed to respond to the needs and wants of patients, then patient satisfaction ratings "go through the roof." Physicians and nursing staff respond to the positive aspirations of patient-centered clinical processes. The perception of quality ripples across the organization and into the community.

4. Medication Error Reduction

The biggest target for immediate quality improvement may be reducing medication errors. In pilot projects for error reduction, Bridge Medical, Inc., has found that hospitals may have at least a 1 percent medication error rate (Davis 2000). Some facilities may err in as many as 3 to 4 percent of all medication transactions, including wrong drug, wrong dose, wrong time, patient allergy, omitted medication, or drug incompatibility with other medications. Drug waste is another form of medication error, as when costly drugs are allowed to expire and are ultimately flushed down the sink by nursing staff or taken off shelves by hospital pharmacists (Lang 2000a).

5. Dedicated Research

Quality experts recommend the creation of a dedicated research organization that can integrate data and manage the process of disseminating information. Douglas Thompson suggests development of an RIID (report, investigate, innovate, and disseminate) unit (Thompson 2000), a cross-functional team similar to quality improvement programs in place in many hospitals and health systems. This approach applies systematic and multi-disciplinary analysis to error reduction, relying on information systems to a much greater extent than traditional quality improvement efforts.

Much more could be done to systematically upgrade clinical quality and reduce clinical variation with greater research and development commitment and resources. Quality experts believe that clinical improvement research is underfunded among hospitals and health systems (Weber 2000a). At California-based Kaiser Permanente, Joe Selby, director of research, gets only $3 million of his $21 million research and development budget from inside the Kaiser system. The Kaiser research and development program is one of the most extensive in the industry, but barely two dozen of the nation's 600 HMOs have an organized health services research program.

At the University of California San Francisco Medical Center, clinicians Robert Wachter, M.D. and colleague Lee Goldman, M.D., were turned down by two foundations and the federal government when they sought research funding to compare the costs and outcomes of inpatient care directed by primary care physicians versus hospitalists. The doctors eventually paid for the evaluation out of their departmental budget and validated the hospitalist concept in an influential article in the *New England Journal of Medicine*.

Multiorganizational collaboratives offer a low-cost, highly practical strategy for harnessing provider organizations in the real work of clinical process improvement. The collaborative approach is encouraged by the Institute for Healthcare Improvement (Lang 2000b). The collaborative approach is a learning laboratory in which participants meet to benchmark performance and share results about what works, in projects lasting six to eight months. Peer-to-peer competition among the participants can be a powerful motivator for improvement, say collaborative organizers. SSM Health Care, a 21-hospital system, has three internal collaboratives in process, with plans for five more. California-based Catholic Healthcare West has 15 of its 46 hospitals participating in an internal collaborative on care of patients with community-acquired pneumonia.

6. Chronic Illness Focus

There is a good reason to focus care management and error reduction programs on chronically ill patients. The right care to the right patient at the right time can be the most cost effective strategy for reforming healthcare in the United States (Rauber 1999). Those with chronic health conditions are the most frequent customers of the nation's $1.3 trillion health system. America spends about $400 billion—one dollar in three—on care of chronically ill patients who are the targets for systematic disease management. Diabetics make up 5 percent of the population but consume 14 percent of all health expenditures. Early identification and management of diabetes can prevent kidney damage, avoiding $70,000 per year for renal dialysis or $100,000 for a kidney transplant.

Health plans are taking aim on chronic conditions. At Cigna, pilot programs in asthma, diabetes, and lower back pain have been so successful they are being expanded nationwide (Rauber 1999). Humana is focusing its care management programs on 40,000 of its 6.2 million enrollees—those at highest risk and whose care will be most expensive—with conditions such as congestive heart failure, asthma, cancer, and neonatal intensive care.

Wellmark Blue Cross and Blue Shield in Iowa has found that 20 percent of its enrollees account for 87 percent of the health plan's medical costs, and just 1 percent of Wellmark's patients were responsible for $465 million of the $1.5 billion the plan spent on healthcare benefits in 2000 (Shulkin 2000). The health plans' challenge is to encourage their networks' physicians to eliminate unexplained clinical variation and consistently follow the best accepted medical practices. Many plans are engaged in extensive profiling of physician performance in managing high-cost conditions. The plans insist they are not exercising economic credentialing, but many insurers and managed care organizations such as Minneapolis-based United HealthCare Corporation are producing care management report cards that advise doctors of where they stand in comparison with national benchmarks. If the health plans are unable to eradicate unexplained clinical variation with voluntary input from providers, Congress may take action to enforce the use of best accepted medical practices.

7. Link to Financial Performance

It is clear from the annual analyses of top hospitals that the payoff from clinical performance improvement is better financial results (Weber 2000a). Intermountain's Dr. Brent James states his organization's case for investing in clinical performance improvement: "Our competitive advantage arises from implementation [of R&D findings]. Because we do the research, we see the results earlier" (Weber 2000a).

At Sutter Health System, chief executive officer Van Johnson, a former Intermountain Health Care executive, earmarked $650,000 to establish the Sutter Health Institute for Research and Education. Sutter's research and development organization is receiving a commitment of 16 percent of the health system's $4 million bottom line last year, with million-dollar funding in future years. Johnson is betting that research and education around clinical improvement will boost his organization's finances, arguing, "we could achieve as much total improvement in the health of this nation from executing consistently what we already know about how to deliver state-of-the-art medical care, as we are likely to receive from all the recent advances in human genetic and pharmaceutical research" (Weber 2000b).

STRATEGIC IMPLICATIONS FOR HOSPITALS, PHYSICIANS, AND HEALTH PLANS

1. *Mobilize for clinical performance improvement.* Clinical performance improvement will be a powerful force in the twenty-first century. It must be one of the top three priorities for management, the medical staff, and the board. Only a long-term, sustained commitment to quality will succeed. Many tools are now available, including benchmarks, pathways, analytic software, computerized databases, and advanced clinical information technology. Invest significant resources, including personnel, capital, and technology. The payoff will be increased efficiency, lower costs per unit of service, and better health outcomes. Data on quality may also become public information.
2. *Focus on errors management.* Start with error reduction. Put a no-fault reporting system into place for nursing and medical staff to

identify errors of all types. Use risk-management experience to set priorities for errors reduction. Deploy analytic software to search for error-suspectible patterns in processes and systems. Benchmark the organization's current performance with peer groups as well as high performers. Keep setting goals higher as performance improves. Keep the board, medical, and nursing staff continuously informed. Reward service units whose error rates improve significantly.

3. *Leadership.* Put a clinically trained executive in charge of clinical performance improvement. Physicians, nurses, pharmacists, and other trained clinicians have the background and training. Research skills and epidemiology training are important assets for these positions. Clinicians also bring the expertise that is essential for respect and communication with their clinical peers. Positions like vice president for quality improvement must be part of the senior management team, reporting directly to the top executives as well as the board.

CONCLUSION

The Institute of Medicine study is a caution light for America's surging $1.3 trillion health industry. Critics warn that hospitalization could be hazardous to your health, noting that in a three-day stay, the odds are one in five that a caregiver will make a mistake that harms a patient (Dutton 2000). Even more alarming is the fact that in the face of estimates that 44,000 to 98,000 deaths may result from medical errors annually, only 655 errors have voluntarily been reported to the Joint Commission since 1995. Insurance executives estimate that fewer than 1 percent of all medical mistakes ever result in a malpractice claim.

Despite the prestige of the Institute of Medicine, many obstacles lie in the path of clinical processes and outcomes improvement. Lack of data, nationally recognized benchmarks, and analytical software are obvious problems. But the most difficult hurdle may be cultural—the "don't ask, don't tell" attitude of many physicians and nurses in the face of errors by their colleagues.

The public's expectations of medicine are simple: Zero defects. Doctors or nurses who commit errors face a potential gauntlet of litigation and adverse publicity that can be career limiting. Today's health system works under the assumption that our caregivers are infallible, and that is the popular expectation. Hospital and medical group managers' expectations are equally high: No mistakes. It is no surprise that hospital workers and doctors tend to hide their mistakes. What is needed is a non-blame environment in which hospitals, physicians, and employees can report mishaps, an action that results in an error-reduction process, rather than a search for the guilty.

According to Brent James, M.D., of Intermountain Health Care, "The shift we have to make is away from this culture of blame. If you pay any attention to the literature at all, you quickly realize that humans are inherently fallible, regardless of training, knowledge and expertise. The only way to prevent errors is to establish systems . . . . The climate must be changed in order to expose and correct problems in a non-blaming environment" (Hagland 2000).

Employers are not waiting for Washington or other organizations to move along remedies to medical errors. In three metropolitan areas, coalitions of major employers are underwriting regional assessments of clinical variation in patterns and costs of care (White 1999). Chicago's Jim Mortimer, president of the Midwest Business Group on Health, notes that *Dartmouth Atlas* data "can raise red flags for employers" by displaying how their markets differ significantly from other similar regions.

Federal regulations that mandate reporting of medical errors are very likely within the near future. Public disclosure is certainly a motivator for change. When hospitals and their physicians are compared side-by-side with their peers and against national benchmarks, the resulting publicity will drive many providers to significantly improve their care management systems.

It is very clear that the United States has the best patient care in the world, but not all patients are receiving it. Reducing clinical variation and medical errors would do much to elevate America's standing in world health comparisons, and to slow the increase in health expenditures.

REFERENCES

Bates, D. W., D. J. Cullen, N. Laird, L. A. Petersen, S. D. Small, D. Servi, G. Laffel, B. J. Sweitzer, B. F. Shea, R. Hallisey, et al. 1995. "Incidence of Adverse Drug Events and Potential Adverse Drug Events. Implications for Prevention." ADE Prevention Study Group. *Journal of the American Medical Association* 274 (1): 29–34.

Benjamin, G. C. 2000. "Addressing Medical Errors: The Key to a Safer Health Care System." *Physician Executive* 26 (2): 66–67.

Brailer, D. J., S. Goldfarb, M. Horzan, F. Katz, R. A. Paulus, and K. Zakrewski. 1996. "Improving Performance with Clinical Decision Support." *Journal on Quality Improvement* 22 (7): 443–56.

Brennan, T. A. 2000. "The Institute of Medicine Report on Medical Errors—Could It Do Harm?" *New England Journal of Medicine* 342 (15): 1123–25.

CareScience. 2000. "Public Report Spurs Mortality Reduction at Borgess Medical Center." (March): 1–4.

Classon, D. C., S. L. Pestotnik, R. S. Evans, J. F. Lloyd, and J. P. Burke. 1997. "Adverse Drug Events in Hospitalized Patients: Excess Length of Stay, Extra Costs, and Attributable Mortality." *Journal of the American Medical Association* 277 (4): 301–06.

Dartmouth Medical School. 2000. *The Dartmouth Atlas of Health Care in the United States.* Chicago: American Hospital Publishing.

Davis, S. 2000. "Quality: Our Business Strategy Using New Technology." CEO Summit, Superior Consultant, Chicago. Presentation materials. October 5. 1–9.

Day, K. L. 2000. "Critical Performance Measures for Wausau Hospital." Rand Healthcare Roundtable, Chicago. Presentation materials. October 27. 1–21.

Dutton, G. 2000. "Do American Hospitals Get Away with Murder?" *Business & Health* 18 (4): 38–47.

Food and Drug Administration. 2001. "Med Error Reports to FDA Show a Mixed Bag." Drug Topics. October 1, 2001. [Online article; retrieved 9/24/03.] http://www.fda.gov/cder/drug/MedErrors/mixed.pdf.

Geniat, E. J., and K. E. Johnson. 2000. *Leadership for a Healthy 21st Century,* 1–28. Chicago: American Hospital Association.

Hagland, M. 2000. "Medical Errors: While the Policy Debate Rages, Clinician Leaders Quietly Push the Healthcare System Toward Quality Improvement." *Physician Performance & Payment Report* 2 (7): 1, 6–10.

Inside Healthcare Computing (IHC) 2000. "VA: Meds System Cut Errors 64% vs. Paper." *Inside Healthcare Computing* 10 (17): 1–2.

Institute of Medicine. 2001. "Crossing the Quality Chasm: A New Health System for the 21st Century." Washington, DC: National Academy of Sciences.

Kohn, L., J. Corrigan, and M. Donaldson. 1999. *To Err Is Human: Building a Safer Health System.* Washington, DC: National Academy Press, Institute of Medicine.

Lang, M. 2000a. "Hospitals Target High-Cost, High-Volume Medications to Achieve Cost Efficiencies." *COR Clinical Excellence* 1 (2): 1–3.

———— 2000b. "Collaboratives Are the Hot Ticket to Success with Performance Improvement Initiatives." *Healthcare Leadership Review* 19 (9): 1.

Lanser, E. G. 2000. "Lessons from the Business Side of Healthcare." *Healthcare Executive* 15 (5): 14–19.

McDonald, C. J., M. Weiner, and S. L. Hui. 2000. "Deaths Due to Medical Errors Are Exaggerated in Institute of Medicine Report." *Journal of the American Medical Association* 284 (1): 93–94.

Moore, J. D., Jr. 1998. "No Answer Book: Atlas Raises Questions About Practice Variations." *Modern Healthcare* 28 (26): 104.

Morrisey, J. 2001. "Clinical-Care IT Still the Final Frontier." *Modern Healthcare* 31 (46): 22–32.

National Coalition on Health Care (NCHC) and Institute for Healthcare Improvement (IHI). 2000. *Reducing Medical Errors and Improving Patient Safety: Success Stories from the Front Lines of Medicine.* Report, February. Washington, DC: NCHC.

O'Keeffe, M. 2000. "Measuring for Success." Rand Healthcare Roundtable. Presentation materials. Chicago. October 27. 1–7.

Rauber, C. 1999. "Disease Management Can Be Good for What Ails Patients and Insurers." *Modern Healthcare* 29 (13): 48–50, 52, 54.

Reeder, L. 2000. "Implementing Performance Improvement in Health Systems." *Healthcare Leadership & Management Report* 8 (7): 1–7.

Rovner, J. 2000. "Washington Wakes Up to Medical Mistakes." *Business & Health* 18 (1): 19.

Shulkin, D. J. 2000. "Commentary: Why Quality Improvement Efforts in Healthcare Fail and What Can Be Done About It." *American Journal of Medical Quality* 15 (2): 49–53.

Solovy, A. 2001. "Healthcare's Most Wired: The Big Payback." *Hospitals & Health Networks* 75 (7): 40–50.

Tedeschi, B. 2000. "No Fun for Sisyphus: The Woes of WebMD and Medscape." *New York Times* October 25, E12.

Thompson, D. 2000. "An Information Systems Strategy for Preventing Medical Errors." *IT Health Strategies* 2 (5): 4.

Weber, D. O. 2000a. "Confronting the R&D Imperative." *Health Forum Journal* 43 (4): 13–15, 60.

———— 2000b. "The View from the Top: What It Takes to Make HCIA's 100 Top Ranking Hospitals." *Strategies for Healthcare Excellence* 13 (7): 1–12.

White, R. 1999. "Projects Aim to Improve Care: Health Data Compared." *Business Insurance* (January): 11.

Zaffrin, S. 2000. "Medication Management: Providing End-to-End Solutions for Healthcare Issues." Superior Consultant, Southfield, Michigan. Presentation materials. October.

Chapter 7

Physician Strategies

> With increasingly compelling evidence that their futures
> are inextricably intertwined, hospitals and physicians
> must aggressively seek new and more creative models for
> working together—models that are grounded in trust and
> shared governance and committed to managing care to
> enhance quality and control costs, not referrals. In this
> volatile and unstable period in the healthcare industry, the
> risks involved with maintaining the status quo or letting
> past failures prevent future collaborations are high.
>
> —Craig E. Holm (2000a)

IT IS IMPOSSIBLE for healthcare organizations to be excellent without
excellent physicians and excellent physician support. Physicians are one
of the most visible components of clinical programs. They provide differentiation through their training, capabilities, and experience and play
a central role in growth, development, and operational success. Yet, in
many instances, physicians are not employees, full or part time, of the
programs and hospitals or health systems with which they are associated.
The nature of relationships between physicians and healthcare organizations ranges from strong and durable to weak and tenuous. Even in situations where physicians are fully integrated within the programs and
organizations they represent, a variety of issues often render these physicians ineffective. How can physician relationships be optimized to support clinical program excellence?

TYPICAL PROBLEMS AND ISSUES

Frequently encountered provider interrelationship problems or issues
include the following:

- *Culture clash.* In its most basic form, collaboration between physicians and healthcare organizations has the potential to result in

culture clash. Physicians and healthcare executives usually have very different backgrounds, strengths, and skills. Successful private practice physicians are autonomous and individualistic; work independently; make decisions quickly; work in small, simple organizations; and may lack business or management training. In contrast, hospitals and health systems are relatively large, complex, bureaucratic organizations, with slow business- and consensus-driven decision making (Holm 2000a). These differences often make meaningful collaboration impossible.

- *Structural incompatibility.* Assuming that hospitals, health systems, and physicians are not all part of one organization (and sometimes even when they are), organizational objectives and economic incentives may differ. In extreme cases, hospitals, health systems, and affiliated physicians may compete broadly for the same business.

- *Inappropriate medical staff involvement.* Many not-for-profit organizations err in the nature of medical staff participation in clinical programs. Rather than identify and put in place different types of roles for various components of the affected medical staff, based on program needs and individual physician capabilities, all or most program roles may be made available to any minimally qualified and interested physician. Not accounting for available physician strengths and skills negates any chance of excellence emerging.

- *Lack of medical staff involvement.* To eliminate the perceived hassles of constructively involving physicians in program development and management, some hospitals and health systems attempt to avoid or minimize physician involvement. While this approach may be expedient and even efficient short term, the centrality of physicians to clinical excellence makes this a flawed strategy. It is impossible to build and sustain excellent programs without meaningful, regular physician participation, input, and direction.

PHYSICIAN CHARACTERISTICS THAT CONTRIBUTE TO PROGRAM EXCELLENCE

Royer (1999) identifies eight clinical characteristics of physicians that can make significant contributions to excellence.

1. *Clinical delivery effectiveness*: Highly developed clinical skills and expertise; continuous drive toward improvement; outstanding outcomes

2. *Service delivery effectiveness*: A high level of service delivery, including kindness and compassion to patients and families; collegial and collaborative behavior with all members of the patient care team

3. *Clinical efficiency*: High productivity and the flexibility and creativity to develop and employ the most efficient care delivery models

4. *Management of resources*: Contribution to new levels of resource use and management, beyond traditional notions of efficiency, to minimize costs; must be able to lead, influence, and involve their peers in these efforts

5. *Teamwork*: Understanding the importance of a team and the ability to facilitate team building and function as a team leader

6. *Teaching*: Student, resident, and staff instruction; mentoring and advancement for those organizations in which educational activities are required or encouraged

7. *Research*: Similar to teaching, for certain organizations; funded research, preparation, presentation, and publication of high-quality papers; collaborative efforts with other researchers

8. *Leadership*: The ability to grow, develop, change, and modify—especially the behaviors of other physicians—often catapults physicians into leadership roles; leadership requires both knowledge-based skills and an array of process-based skills (see Figures 7.1 and 7.2)

Physicians who will be involved in a central role in program development and management must possess most of these characteristics and competencies; a few, such as leadership and teamwork, are especially critical to success. Physicians involved more peripherally should have clinical and service-delivery capabilities that distinguish them from the vast majority of other practicing physicians.

FOSTERING ENTREPRENEURSHIP

One area not identified by Royer is entrepreneurship. Historically, physicians have been extremely entrepreneurial in developing their own practices and businesses. For physicians in solo or small group practices—typical until the past ten years—it was "sink or swim" businesswise, and few medical practices sunk. Physicians demonstrated an aptitude for cultivating patients and referrals that allowed their revenue streams to grow up to, and occasionally beyond, their capacity to handle patient volumes. These successful practices were aided by a shortage of physicians in most

Figure 7.1   Knowledge-Based Leadership Skills Criteria

1. Grasp of mission and having an understanding of
   - Importance
   - Balance
   - Interdigitation
   - New concepts
     - Customer-focused clinical services
     - Distributed education
     - Right-sized education
     - Translation research
   - Need to be a "flag waver"

2. Managed care issues
   - Style of practice
   - Reimbursement issues associated with capitation
   - Surviving in the schizophrenic environment of fee for service and capitation

3. Understanding of and ability to implement a sound performance appraisal process that parallels salary adjustment

4. Understanding of and ability to implement compensation menu

5. Understanding of and comfort with reengineering, redesigning, and change process

6. Understanding of specific system departmental/regional/group issues

7. Understanding of system/department/region/group's future direction

8. Understanding of how to bring department/region to "world class" status

Source: Royer, T. C. 1999. "Measuring Physician Performance." In *Clinical Resource and Quality Management,* edited by S. B. Ransom and W. W. Pinsky, 136–37. Tampa, FL: American College of Physician Executives.

specialties and geographic areas and by fairly robust insurance coverage continuously spurring demand increases.

The experience in physician entrepreneurship in clinical program development and management is much more varied. Even in academic medical centers where the physicians are more connected to the organization than

Figure 7.2   Process-Based Leadership Skills

- Firm and fair
- Collaborative and collegial
- Willing to admit mistakes
- Well focused and able to maintain directions regardless of peripheral conversations
- Good listener
- Consensus builder
- Ability to make decisions
- "Glass half-full" person
- Charismatic leader and speaker
- Can relate to present staff (diversity/internal leaders)
- Can handle difficult issues
- Outcome oriented

Source: Royer, T. C. 1999. "Measuring Physician Performance." In *Clinical Resource and Quality Management,* edited by S. B. Ransom and W. W. Pinsky, 136–37. Tampa, FL: American College of Physician Executives.

in community-based healthcare institutions, entrepreneurship is highly variable. Some feel that physicians attracted to academic medical centers and to large organizations generally are more risk averse and less entrepreneurial than the mainstream, while others believe that it is a function of economic incentives or the lack thereof. Both factors probably contribute to a disappointing (from the perspective of the hospital or healthcare system) level of physician enthusiasm, energy, and leadership in clinical program growth overall to date.

Nonetheless, cases of exemplary physician entrepreneurship abound. While financial incentives can spur entrepreneurial behavior, most of what has occurred in healthcare appears to be driven by a physician or group of physicians who want to be at the forefront of care delivery. Such physicians realize that the development of clinically advanced, outstanding, and distinctive programs requires collaboration among multiple providers. These physicians seek to participate in a level of clinical capability that exceeds what they can develop on their own, thus requiring cooperation and collaboration with others. They also understand the central role that physician leaders can play in such endeavors and position themselves to drive program development.

In these settings, physician entrepreneurs can be and often are as aggressive and goal driven as their predecessors were in building private practices in the late twentieth century. Physician entrepreneurs in such settings provide a primary source of new ideas for growth and development, keep abreast of emerging technological breakthroughs and reimbursement challenges, and assist in motivating the entire team continuously to achieve new levels of excellence.

The experience of Mercy Medical Center in Canton, Ohio, is a good illustration of what is possible with physician entrepreneurship. Mercy brought on Dr. Ahmed Sabe to head its heart center in 1999. Dr. Sabe began implementing a variety of service extensions and enhancements, the most innovative of which was emergency cardiac catheterization in the emergency department. He also worked on improving the heart center's operations and facilities to provide exceptional service to staff and referring physicians and patients and their families. Equally important was his dedication to quality and a nonstop effort to raise Mercy's performance levels above that of any other hospital in Ohio and elevate Mercy to the top rank nationally. As a result, Mercy's heart program was awarded one of the first center-of-excellence designations from the federal government.

ASSUMING MANAGEMENT RESPONSIBILITIES

Equally important to successful program development and operation is the ability of physician leaders to assume management responsibilities and carry them out well. Royer's (1999) profile of physician characteristics and leadership skill requirements include many aspects of the management challenge for physicians.

- *Physicians must want to take on management roles and responsibilities.* This point may sound obvious, but it is vital. Physicians may be promoted, formally or informally, into these positions without the interest and enthusiasm to take on the roles and responsibilities they assume. This situation is hardly unusual in healthcare or in the general business community where the stars of the organization may get promoted beyond their management capabilities and interests. The capacity to carry out well these roles and responsibilities starts with interest and enthusiasm, but does not end there.
- *Physicians will need management training, education, and support.* Few physicians will advance to these roles with already-developed capaci-

ties. In nearly every instance, formal training and education is necessary and must be built into the development plan. Support from other elements of the organization is also mandatory—both formally through mentoring and education and informally through the myriad communications that occur, which can be perceived as indicating confidence in and approval of the physicians' performance.

- *Physician managers will need financial responsibility and accountability.* Far too frequently, physicians are placed in figurehead leadership positions, with some responsibility and authority, but often without any financial responsibility or accountability. At a minimum, physician managers must be charged with some control over program-related finances, especially direct and indirect expenses. Better yet is full budget development and management responsibility, covering both expenses and revenues. Rarer still, but even more desirable, is full financial accountability for budget performance, ensuring that positive variances from budget carry rewards (both financial and nonfinancial) and negative variances carry consequences.

RECRUITING "TOP DOCS"

Nothing will catapult a clinical program faster from the ordinary to the outstanding than bringing in new clinical stars. It can take years or sometimes decades to home grow the clinical expertise necessary to make a program first rate. By employing a "buy" versus "make" strategy, rapid, overnight improvement is possible. And, increasingly, physicians are demonstrating the kind of mobility that has been common in the general business community for years but was unheard of in healthcare until recently.

A.I. DuPont Hospital for Children provides a graphic illustration of this strategy. DuPont Hospital was established as a pediatric orthopedic and rehabilitation hospital and only began the transition to a full-service general pediatric hospital in 1976. With the disadvantage of a relatively small natural market (the state of Delaware) of its own and extremely formidable competition to the north in Philadelphia and to the south in Baltimore—but with the extraordinary resources of the Nemours Foundation to draw on—the hospital was able to jump-start its development in a number of clinical areas. Most notable was the recruitment of world-renowned pediatric cardiothoracic surgeon Dr. William Norwood and a team of nearly 40 of his associates from Switzerland in the late 1990s.

Dr. Norwood's arrival put the DuPont Hospital's heart program on the map, changing it from a good community resource into a national and international center of excellence. It also immediately established a strong academic orientation to this program, since Dr. Norwood's team brought with it a number of research projects in process and the capacity to be a research powerhouse in pediatric cardiothoracic surgery for this affiliate of Thomas Jefferson Medical College.

Recruiting physician stars from one organization to another has been somewhat common in academic settings for years. Historically, the impetus for this approach has been primarily academic rather than clinical—as academic centers attempted to increase their standing among their peers, acquiring established researchers with already-existing grant funding and the potential for more has been an accepted way to advance individual departments and institutions. Today, it is not unusual for groups of academic stars to pick up and move whole sections and even departments at once, as the DuPont example attests.

Clinical revenues became larger and more important to academic medical centers in the last 30 years, but physician stature and income in academic centers was still largely a function of research standing and funding rather than clinical excellence and revenues. As a result, some excellent physicians migrated from academic-based practice to community practice. In community settings, physician incomes could be maximized and, away from the slow-moving bureaucracy of academic institutions, clinical programs often could be advanced more successfully.

One of the most significant examples of this increasingly common movement away from academic medical centers is the heart center at Saint Joseph's Hospital of Atlanta in Georgia. The impetus for the development of this center in the 1980s came from physicians who were formerly associated with Emory University. As it became possible to have a first-rate community hospital heart center and with a desire to provide excellent care in a private practice setting, a number of the Emory cardiac "stars" left and set up their practices at Saint Joseph's. The hospital's program grew into one of the ten largest in the United States, was a lead participant in the first Medicare heart bypass demonstration project, and has been repeatedly recognized as one of the top cardiovascular hospitals in the United States.

Community-based physicians have been extremely stable and reluctant to relocate. Although there has always been some mobility within large metropolitan areas, even that has been quite limited until the past few years. Now, however, community-based physicians, too, are the subject of bidding wars, as hospitals and health systems strive to bring these top docs into their clinical program development.

Where is it all going? The competition for the best physicians to lead or support clinical program development shows no signs of abating. As the impetus for excellence grows, the war for the best talent should only escalate. The surest way to stand out from the pack in an increasingly crowded and busy market is to offer the best talent.

The next frontier is moving from perceived quality and excellence based on reputation alone to a combination of tangible measures, involving both outcomes and service. Tomorrow's top docs will be able to prove they are the best through superior outcomes and high customer satisfaction ratings.

Another challenge for hospitals and health systems in the future will be not just getting top doctors in the front door, but retaining them. As mobility increases and the bidding wars escalate, financial incentives will be necessary but not sufficient. Professional satisfaction and enrichment are more important factors in retention as other professions, such as nursing, demonstrate. Hospitals and health systems must provide an environment that emphasizes and preferably optimizes physicians' professional development and satisfaction.

ALLIANCES WITH "BRANDED" ACADEMIC CENTERS

An increasingly common method of creating outstanding, distinctive programs and augmenting medical staff capabilities is through alliances with strong academic medical centers and other "branded" specialty hospitals. These alliances take a variety of forms, ranging from loose marketing arrangements to formal management contracts, including the tertiary center providing physician and operational, financial, and marketing support to the affiliate.

For example, many of the larger and most well-regarded cancer centers in the United States, including M.D. Anderson Cancer Center and Memorial Sloan-Kettering Cancer Center, have created networks of affiliates and forged various relationships with them. The most basic relationship is a loose affiliation in which the community hospital or healthcare system enters into a contract that allows for the use of the tertiary center's name as an affiliate and generally involves participation in some of the clinical studies or protocols that originate from the cancer center.

A second and somewhat greater level of affiliation involves actual physician participation in care delivery at the site of the community affiliate, generally in the form of one or more regularly scheduled subspecialty clinics. A third and deeper level of affiliation involves direct provision of service by the tertiary center on an ongoing basis at the community site. The latter could involve staffing a radiation therapy center, providing a medical director and other staff, or at the extreme, operating an outpatient cancer center as a franchise of the tertiary center. In nearly all of these arrangements, the community hospital or healthcare system is able to realize tangible benefits from the outstanding reputation of its tertiary partner and often can provide services in its community that would otherwise be difficult, if not impossible, to offer, featuring physicians who are extremely well trained and subspecialized.

Many of the outstanding children's hospitals in the United States have created similar types of arrangements with community affiliates. Children's Hospital of Denver provides specialty clinics to a huge geographic area, extending throughout Colorado and into Wyoming. Children's Hospital of Wisconsin has similar arrangements all over the state of Wisconsin. And, taking such arrangements to yet another level, Children's Hospital of Philadelphia manages a pediatric inpatient unit within some of its community affiliates. Finally, children's hospitals are pioneers in the use of telemedicine as a means of creating new-age links between their tertiary centers and many of the remote affiliates and communities they serve.

Alliances with branded academic centers and other tertiary hospitals are not always successful, nor are they a panacea for weak or ailing clinical programs. However, as these and other examples illustrate, they can augment and strengthen community healthcare organizations in a variety of ways. Most obvious is the marketing benefit from association with a leading, recognized brand. Probably of greater importance long term are the benefits from star—or at least stellar—physician support, including the potential to bring new services to community sites, offering a higher level of capabilities in the community and supporting local physicians and others to enhance clinical services.

In situations where a more substantive affiliation is established, infrastructure support in operations and finance can be critical to program success. Lastly, these alliances can assist in jump-starting or expediting initial and ongoing program development.

Health First, an integrated delivery system located on Florida's east coast, created a new relationship with Shands Hospital and the University of Florida College of Medicine to assist in getting its first center of excellence off the ground. The affiliation resulted in Shands and the University of Florida providing a medical director for Health First's emerging heart institute. The new medical director was a neutral party who could help bring the diverse cardiovascular medical practices together with the Health First hospitals into one unified entity. The link back to Shands and the University of Florida also ensures that the latest clinical research is immediately available and integrated, where appropriate, into Health First's heart center.

Another twist on these relationships involves broad-based affiliations across a number of departments and clinical programs between the community hospital and its academic partner. Holy Cross Hospital, a community hospital on Chicago's South Side, selected University of Illinois Medical Center, also in Chicago, as its academic medical center affiliate. In the first manifestation of the new relationship, University of Illinois contracted with Holy Cross to provide anesthesiology coverage. The two organizations are also reviewing potential relationships for other hospital-based services as well as collaborative efforts for the initial clinical centers Holy Cross Hospital is in the process of developing.

BUILDING A BASE OF PHYSICIAN REFERRALS

Physicians are a primary, if not *the* primary, customer of clinical programs. While consumer groups are also important, as are managed care plans in some markets, gaining and maintaining physician referrals is a cornerstone of program success. The ability to attract and then continue to satisfy referring physicians cannot be assumed to be a simple matter or taken for granted. Strong, ongoing marketing efforts and excellent supporting operations must be in place.

As clinical programs grow and develop, the business development challenge often changes from a local market area to a regional, or in some cases state or multistate, market area. Sometimes, clinical program development attempts to target a large geographic area from the outset. Occasionally, a provider will skip over the local market because of extreme competition and focus on the more extended market initially. Whatever the target market, clinical program development success demands careful, thoughtful, and creative cultivation of referring physicians.

Fundamental to successful marketing to referring physicians is offering a quality product. Too often, healthcare organizations embark on ambitious marketing programs without really having a product to sell or before the clinical program is ready to be offered to a broader market.

Failing to actually deliver a good, if not outstanding, service can seriously derail clinical program development and undermine the confidence of referring physicians in the organization's clinical program for many years. And today, both the service itself and the communication with referring physicians must be very good. Unless both components are up to par, cultivation of a broad base of referring physicians is not possible.

Another common problem, and the opposite of that cited above, is failure to roll out the marketing program even after the product and support system are quite well developed. In the past, word-of-mouth marketing was sufficient to build the physician referral base. In some academic medical centers, purposeful cultivation of physician referrals is still viewed as unseemly. Either because of arrogance or ignorance, an excellent clinical program could fail to find a market or keep one because of inadequate referral physician outreach.

A large teaching and referral hospital in the East had an outstanding pediatric program and children's hospital within a hospital for many years. In fact, up until the mid-1990s, it was essentially the only game in town and the region. However, most of the other providers in the state began to merge into large systems. Two of these systems were able to develop competing children's hospitals with new facilities and a number of new outstanding physicians. As the new kids on the block, these systems were aggressive about cultivating referrals. They drew on the existing referral bases both within their newly formed systems as well as key physician sources outside their systems. With large investments to recover and with a catch-up mentality, the two systems and their new children's hospitals needed to run faster, harder, and smarter. After two years of operation, they had significantly undercut their long-standing rival's referral base. In this period, inpatient volumes dropped by 25 percent and key outpatient services were down about 10 percent at the established program. By year five of the start-ups' operations, both were financially viable and thriving, while the established pediatric program was essentially on life support.

What lessons can be drawn from these organizations?

- A quality program must be developed, maintained, and continuously improved.
- Referring physicians are a key customer, if not the key customer, for any sophisticated, complex clinical center.

- Cultivation of referring physicians must be part of early operations, but also an ongoing emphasis of the clinical program.
- Although the services themselves must be outstanding, equally important is the quality of the referring physician communications.
- Competitors are emerging and existing competitors are upgrading their programs continuously; therefore, do not take a strong competitive position for granted.

RELATIONSHIPS WITH KEY AFFILIATED PHYSICIANS AND GROUPS

Beyond marketing and cultivation of referrals, any strong clinical center is dependent on a solid base of local cooperating, participating physicians. The more complex and comprehensive the program, the larger and more diverse the home physician base must be. In most clinical program development today, the size and scope of the local physician base can and should continue to grow for years, as additional opportunities to increase the breadth and depth of the programs emerge. To make this more explicit, Figure 7.3 compares a typical undifferentiated, community-based neurology and neurosurgery services center with a second-generation, community-based neurosciences center.

Individual physicians or groups may participate in a variety of different ways in clinical program development and operation. At one extreme, physicians may function in an exclusively private practice mode, participating as they have traditionally in the care of their private patients within the affected disciplines—as a referral source or consulting physician at arm's length from the program—and in various advisory capacities on committees as they do on the general medical staff.

At the opposite end of the spectrum are highly integrated mechanisms including joint ventures, employment, and financial risk sharing arrangements. In between these extremes is an extensive range of other affiliation alternatives, the most common of which are contractual relationships involving medical directorates or subdirectorates and various other management and professional service contract relationships involving all, a large part, or some smaller, definable part of a program.

Figure 7.4 illustrates these alternatives and highlights how they compare relative to the degree of collaboration entailed in any of the options. Collaboration generally includes three main factors: economic interdependence, operational integration, and control. The greater the collaboration,

Figure 7.3   Neurosciences Development Plan

Initial Properties	Second Round	Later
◆ Stroke ◆ Trauma ◆ Spine/back ◆ Multiple sclerosis ◆ Seizure disorders	◆ Cognitive disorders ◆ Headache ◆ Movement disorders ◆ Neuromuscular ◆ Neurooncology	◆ Balance disorders ◆ Neuropsychiatry ◆ Sleep disorders ◆ Visual disorders

YEAR   1 ——————— 3 ——————— 5 ———————→

Source: Health Strategies & Solutions, Inc. 2003. Used with permission.

the more economically and operationally integrated the parties. The third factor, less frequently mentioned but at least as important, is control. The greater the integration, the less control and influence any party has unless it is clearly the dominant partner. In less integrated models, all parties can exert much more control over their own operations and destiny, although, obviously, their sphere of influence is much smaller than the collective sphere.

CONCLUSION

This chapter has addressed the primary subject of strategies to build stronger relationships between physicians and healthcare organizations to contribute to clinical distinctiveness, especially within individual clinical programs. As previous chapters have indicated, physician stars and leaders become a consumer magnet as well, and are increasingly important in the emerging consumer-choice era.

The subject of physician relationships and structures is a critical topic in healthcare today. Holm (2000a, 2000b) and others have written extensively on physician–healthcare organization relationships and should be referred to for a more complete review of this subject.

As with other aspects of the physician strategies, organizations cannot assume that creating positive, mutually beneficial relationships with key physicians and groups will naturally evolve. These critical relationships

Figure 7.4   Physician–Health System Collaboration Alternatives

Model	Degree of Collaboration
◆ Independence ◆ Practice support ◆ Real estate partnership ◆ Management contract ◆ Joint operating agreement ◆ Economic joint venture ◆ Employment/practice acquisition ◆ Whole program joint venture	Minimal ↕ Extensive

Source: Health Strategies & Solutions, Inc. 2003. Used with permission.

require ongoing, thoughtful, and creative attention. Affiliated physicians must be

- cultivated as key customers;
- included as part of the "team" to the extent they are willing and able to be;
- encouraged to constructively critique operations and progress;
- solicited for advice regarding future development needs and priorities; and
- considered formal participants in more integrated relationships if interested and if these relationships can be structured in mutually beneficial ways.

REFERENCES

Holm, C. E. 2000a. *Next Generation Physician–Health System Partnerships*. Chicago: Health Administration Press.

———. 2000b. "Physician Issues" column. Series in *Journal of Healthcare Management*. 45:2–6.

Royer, T. C. 1999. "Measuring Physician Performance." In *Clinical Resource and Quality Management*, edited by S. B. Ransom and W. W. Pinsky. Tampa, FL: American College of Physician Executives.

Chapter 8

World-Class Service

> Customers want to be treated nicely. They want a hassle-free, reasonably priced experience. And they want their problems fixed . . . All good service companies attempt to be good at all three dimensions of quality. The very best service companies, however, endeavor to be as good as the competition in two dimensions of service quality, and better than anyone else in the world in one.

—*Tim Mannello (2000)*

ACROSS AMERICA, HOSPITALS and physician organizations are discovering how imperative service is to their success, taking lessons from top companies like Nordstrom, Inc., Marriott Corporation, Southwest Airlines, and the Ritz-Carlton Hotel Company (Dow and Cook 1997). New Jersey's Hackensack University Medical Center is clothing its patients in designer wear by Nicole Miller, abandoning "moonie" gowns as hopelessly anticonsumer (Press Ganey 2002). Giving patients best-in-class service leads to higher volumes and revenues, repeat customers, word-of-mouth advertising, and even shorter lengths of stay. Hospitals that emphasize service are not only out-competing rivals—some patient magnets like Houston's M.D. Anderson Cancer Center are full every day.

Customer satisfaction feedback is used to improve quality, identify process bottlenecks, and motivate managers and staff. Virtually every hospital today monitors patient satisfaction levels and many track the morale and working environment of staff as well. Customer satisfaction research services use mail surveys, telephone interviews, and Internet questionnaires to probe post-service satisfaction, from the emergency department to the critical care unit.

GIVING PATIENTS WHAT THEY WANT

Consumers are becoming empowered to make choices, especially those insured by government programs. Medicare patients have many choices, and most hospitals and physicians also accept Medicaid. Insured patients can select from a wide array of healthcare providers and treatments, with few limits. Commercial health insurance customers can go where they want for health services. Managed care plans have virtually abandoned the gatekeeper concept, and prior authorization programs are afraid of offending doctors or their patients, or fear being sued for denial of access. Customer-friendly preferred provider organizations (PPOs) typically offer a broad choice of hospitals and doctors. The result is that most managed care patients can refer themselves to virtually any healthcare institution or physician in the marketplace.

Quality counts, but in the absence of data on quality outcomes, consumers are often forced to rely on recommendations of friends or other providers. Very often, it is service quality—not clinical quality—that determines consumer choice. Today's consumers are informed, demanding, often skeptical. Recent consumer rankings revealed hospitals scoring even lower than the post office in customer satisfaction (ASCI 2002).

What do patients want? They may be sick, in pain, or chronically ill, but they are still consumers. Healthcare is a service industry. Patients are no different than car buyers or hotel guests. They judge the quality of service against the following three dimensions:

1. Customer intimacy—personal sensitivity and responsiveness of staff
2. Efficiency and cost-effectiveness—prompt attention and value pricing
3. Service superiority—consistently exceeding competitors

Customer satisfaction creates customer loyalty. These highly pleased consumers will become repeat business, recommend to others, and may become philanthropic donors. According to a widely read *Harvard Business Review* article, "Why Satisfied Customers Defect" (Jones and Sasser 1995), managers should be concerned, not pleased, if the majority of their customers rate themselves as "satisfied" as opposed to "completely satisfied." Most businesses invest far more in marketing to obtain customers than they spend on keeping the ones they have. The Bayer Corporation, a market research organization that works with managed care plans, reports that HMOs may spend $200 to $500 to acquire a new member but spend less than 20 percent of that amount for member retention (Wood 1996).

THE BEST CARE, NO MATTER WHAT

Quality matters. Hospitals with high levels of patient satisfaction recognize the strong link between pleasing customers and volume, reputation, staffing, and profitability. A national study of one million patient questionnaires identified those issues rated most important by healthcare consumers (Press Ganey 1999). Interpersonal concerns and being informed critically influence patients' perceptions. Patients care more about what is done to them and what is told to them than any other factor. Happy patients, in turn, mean higher profits. Patient satisfaction is strongly linked to a growing bottom line. A study of 550 hospitals found that the highest-scoring hospitals on patient satisfaction were also the most profitable.

PLANETREE MODEL OF PATIENT-CENTERED CARE

Planetree, an innovative model of patient-centered care, was launched in San Francisco in 1978 by a determined group of consumer advocates. Named for the site where Hippocrates taught the first medical students, Planetree sought to make consumers the center of the health system. Planetree's first patient resource center was established in the former medical library of Pacific Medical Center. Hundreds of books and journals were compiled for patient education by a librarian who had worked at the National Library of Medicine.

Planetree's first model facility, a 13-bed medical/surgical unit at Pacific Medical Center, broke new ground. Furnishings were homelike, with curtains at the windows and carpeted hallways. In a radical departure, the nursing station was eliminated, replaced by decentralized clinical workstations. Planetree patients had open access to their own medical records and could enter their own patient progress notes.

Today, more than 35 facilities have implemented Planetree principles. Griffin Hospital in Derby, Connecticut, is a leading example of Planetree concepts and now hosts the national offices for the Planetree organization. Griffin replaced its hospital in the 1990s based on Planetree principles and created an exemplary patient-pleasing facility that increased its market share more than 15 percent.

The combination of patient-centered facilities and service paid off in superior patient satisfaction ratings. Griffin's Press Ganey ratings are in the 99th percentile and its volume has soared 18 percent (Bank 2001). The senior management team of Griffin Hospital—chief executive officer; chief operating officer; and the vice presidents for medical affairs, patient care, and human resources—still meet weekly to review complaints and look for opportunities for process improvement.

BUILDING A SERVICE CULTURE

Customer service is an "idea in good currency" that fits perfectly into today's consumer-led healthcare market. Placing a high priority on consumer satisfaction is getting strong encouragement from the Joint Commission, Institute of Medicine, National Quality Forum, Institute for Healthcare Improvement, and Leapfrog Group. Hospitals today are monitoring their patient satisfaction levels. Some have years of data, and a body of evidence is growing in support of quality improvement that results in satisfied patients.

Building a culture of customer service is a goal of the Military Health System (MHS), one of the best untold stories of patient satisfaction in the United States. The MHS Survey of Inpatient Care found that military inpatients reported 30 percent fewer problems, when compared to civilian hospital averages (Carrato 2001). The Department of Defense (DOD) TRICARE program employs managed care to provide health services to military beneficiaries, including dependents and retirees. TRICARE uses a comprehensive healthcare survey of Department of Defense beneficiaries. Nearly nine of ten DOD beneficiaries had no problems with courtesy and helpfulness of military treatment staff, according to an annual survey. Customer service in military and TRICARE contractor facilities is benchmarked against other hospitals and managed care plans using data from the *Annual National Research Corporation Healthcare Market Guide*.

Physicians are also learning that it pays to satisfy their patients. Some health plans are incentivizing physician groups with bonus payments for higher levels of consumer satisfaction and member re-enrollment. Aetna is experimenting with bonuses of up to 3 percent to capitated medical groups, based on analysis of more than one million satisfaction surveys from health plan members (Larkin 1999). Blue Cross of California has switched its physician incentives from cost cutting to bonuses now based exclusively on customer satisfaction (Jackson 2001).

LINKING SERVICE-LINE MANAGEMENT AND PATIENT SATISFACTION

Intense service-line competition is occurring among providers. Cardiology, cancer, and women's health are the leading centers of excellence, with growing interest in neurosciences, orthopedic surgery, and emergency services as the focal points of market strategy. Patient satisfaction is a key factor in growing a successful service line. The Health Care Advisory Board's Cardiovascular Roundtable identified patient satisfaction as the top priority. Press Ganey provides DRG-specific indicators of customer satisfaction (Lanser 2001).

Service-line managers can link patient satisfaction data to clinical pathways to optimize clinical performance and connect the dots between quality, cost, and satisfaction to improve performance, especially for high-volume and high-profit DRGs. Patient satisfaction information can be added to other key management data such as clinical path variances, length of stay, readmission rates, nosocomial infections, and costs for specific DRGs.

In the focused factories of clinical centers of excellence described by Regina Herzlinger (1997) of the Harvard Business School, the majority of patients are highly predictable in their health status, demands, even their hopes and fears. Yet the challenge for every hospital and health professional is that each patient expects to be treated individually. In healthcare, Herzlinger's factory metaphor represents an industrial model, which may be highly successful in cost efficiency but could have the unwelcome effect of making customers feel like a number.

Mass customization uses technology and service personalization to provide an experience that is based on personal respect, emotional sensitivity, and the ability to modify standards to meet individual needs. At one Midwest hospital, every inpatient is asked what are the three most important things their caregivers should know. Patient responses are posted on white-boards above the patients' beds. Some patient demands include the following:

- "Take care of my wife."
- "Don't touch me without telling me what you are doing."
- "Don't wake me when I'm sleeping."
- "I am afraid of pain."

BENCHMARKING WITH THE BEST

Providers seeking to improve service can take lessons from industry leaders. Benchmark data are available to healthcare organizations by participating in ongoing satisfaction research programs with comparative data by peer group and national averages. Leading providers organize their customer services very specifically to their patient populations in terms of demographics, severity and complexity, payer mix, expectations, and level of knowledge about their condition.

Hospital quality is good, even very good, in the eyes of most patients. Some 85 percent of ambulatory consumers, on average, rank their patient care experiences as good or very good on a five-point measurement scale (Mylod 2002). On average, only 1.4 percent of patients of the hospitals in the lowest 10th percentile scored their ambulatory care as very poor, while hospitals in the highest 10th percentile get top scores of very good from 78.7 percent of their consumers.

National and peer-group satisfaction data can be used as benchmarks for assessment of performance. Some hospitals group their good and very good scores into a satisfied customer rating of positive satisfaction, but clustering scores may hide problems. A composite satisfied score of 90 percent may occur when 60 percent rate their satisfaction at very good, while another 30 percent rated their care good. But just the reverse—30 percent very good, 60 percent good—suggests a very different satisfaction experience. Some hospitals focus primarily on the very good scores as a better measure of the highest-level satisfaction.

OPEN ACCESS REVOLUTIONIZES PATIENT SCHEDULING

A radical innovation in customer service—called open access or advanced access—is breaking backlogs in physician offices and providing on-demand access for consumers. Patients love it, and so do their physicians. Open access gives physicians the ability to completely change their schedule at the last minute, as late as 7:30 A.M. on a day when the first patient is scheduled for 8 A.M. One enthusiastic healthcare executive, U.S. Air Force Captain F. Thomas Siskron (2002), believes that other providers "will be able to discover what we have discovered . . . the joy of delivering absolutely world-class appointment access with near infinite flexibility in providers' schedules." In a variety of physician offices and medical clinics, both civilian and military, open access has been tried and evaluated extensively, with positive results such as the following:

- An overall wait time of three days or less
- On-demand access to care
- Compliance rate of 99 percent of patients keeping appointments

- Up to a 50 percent reduction in no-shows, cancellations, and walk-ins
- Physicians and staff can go to lunch on time and leave on time

The concept of open access addresses a problem common to many physician offices and ambulatory care clinics: waiting weeks for next appointments and walk-in service that may require patients to wait for hours. When most demand for access from today is scheduled into the future, it naturally creates a reservoir, or backlog, of patient demand. Daily schedules, which have been booked by demand from up to four weeks ago, are saturated well in advance. On top of seeing a full schedule of patients who have been waiting days or weeks for their appointments, providers must respond to walk-in acute demand as well.

The secret to open access is to recognize that the number of appointments that providers see each day is nearly equal to the number that patients actually request. Open access "tears down the dam and lets the river of demand flow naturally" (Siskron 2002). Healthcare is a service industry that is governed by the laws of supply and demand. The potential demand for office visits can be predicted, based on the size and demographics of the population, and clinic capacity can be calculated, based on the number and efficiencies of the providers. Open access assumes demand is relatively constant from day to day and aligns patients to same-day service rather than rationing appointments by scheduling them days, weeks, or even months ahead.

The concept of open access is still being refined. Since more patients tend to show up in physician offices early in the week, after waiting over the weekend, some practices and clinics overstaff on Mondays and Tuesdays or extend hours in anticipation of higher caseloads. In actuality, offices using open access are learning they only need to meet about 75 percent of demand on a same-day basis, because 25 percent will be "good backlog" that is appropriately scheduled into the future. The simplicity of open access is recognizing that fluctuations in demand will even out over the days, weeks, and months.

SERVICE GUARANTEES

Customer-centered hospitals are beginning to promise consumer satisfaction—a hospital will adjust the bill, or even write it off when triage or medical attention is not given promptly. Emergency department patients at the CentraState Medical Center in Freehold, New Jersey, have a 15/30 guarantee: the program guarantees that every patient will see a nurse within 15 minutes and a doctor with 30 minutes, or the hospital pays the bill (Gutter and Marinaro 2002). The 15/30 guarantee has been so successful that it has been adopted by seven of the eight hospitals in the Robert Wood Johnson Health System and Network of New Jersey.

Service guarantees are even being offered in busy trauma units. A service promise is being made by the emergency department (ED) of the Robert Wood Johnson (RWJ) Medical Center, which operates a Level-1 trauma center in New Brunswick, New Jersey (Keenan 2000). In the past, patients arriving at RWJ's emergency department would wait at least 15 minutes just registering to be seen. Now, patients are seen immediately by a floating triage nurse, who escorts them to the fast-track treatment area. Physician staffing has also been rearranged to provide for higher physician availability during the ED's busiest hours each day. ED staff were cross-trained to improve efficiency and service without adding staff.

SERVICE TRAINING

To meet the universal need for customer service training and orientation, companies are creating a variety of online tools and web-based learning programs for healthcare organizations. Atlanta-based Greystone.net is launching a web-enabled set of more than 20 educational programs for managers and frontline employees. Educational modules are available around the clock so participants can learn at their own pace.

Management development programs include interviewing skills, coaching peak performance, developing a service culture, and management strategies for recruitment and retention. Greystone.net is an application service provider, so hospitals and health systems pay only for the license and number of slots needed to provide their managers access to the tools, data, and programs.

Internet-based customer satisfaction and employee retention programs like Greystone.net offer a variety of educational modules, tools for performance improvement, benchmark data, and online communications, including the following (Peterson 2002):

- E-learning courses for managers and employees (e.g., telephone courtesy, complaint handling, coaching and counseling)
- Virtual toolbox for performance improvement (e.g., checklists, surveys, team exercises)
- Executive communications that can be customized (e.g., building a service culture, sending the service message)

- Opinion research tools (e.g., customized surveys)
- Benchmark data (e.g., quarterly opinion surveys, national databases)
- Employee recognition (e.g., web-based welcomes for new employees, recognition for service contributions)
- Industry best practices (e.g., proven strategies, case studies)
- Customer satisfaction data (e.g., reference data, client-customized performance data)
- Network communications among managers addressing service issues

Case Study in Patient Dissatisfaction: Emergency Departments

A hospital's front door is the emergency department; many hospitals experience 35 to 60 percent of their admissions through the ED. On a national basis, emergency departments are experiencing a capacity crisis. In Houston, Boston, and South Florida, a growing number of EDs are on diversion and cannot handle additional patients.

The ED capacity problem is making the traditional problem of long waits in noisy, crowded waiting rooms even worse. As a result, a growing number of hospitals are making the ED their highest priority for improving patient satisfaction. Some hospitals provide beepers to patients, allowing them go to the cafeteria or find a quiet corner until the emergency physician is ready to see them. Kimball Medical Center in Lakewood, New Jersey, even gives its patients a box lunch when waits may be long and keeps a refreshment cart available to waiting ED consumers (Press Ganey 2002).

Saint Barnabas Medical Center in Livingston, New Jersey, was the number one emergency department in patient satisfaction in 2001, among the highest-volume departments (over 40,000 visits per year) of the more than 400 EDs that use Press Ganey surveys to rate consumer service levels (Saint Barnabas 2000). The department's "door-to-door drug time"—the amount of time it takes for heart attack patients to receive clot-busting drugs from the time they enter the ED—is 15 minutes.

Lack of communication is a primary factor in patient dissatisfaction in the emergency department, believes Mary Malone (2002), executive director of consulting services for Press Ganey. Miscommunication can be a major contributor to malpractice litigation. Malone cites that failures of provider-patient communication may be responsible for as much as 60 percent of medical tort cases.

Frequent and candid communication is the top demand of patients in emergency departments. A study of one million ED patients reveals that communication and courtesy are the most important patient expectations (Gesell 2000). Patients cited the following as their top concerns:

- Staff care about me as a person
- I am kept well informed about delays
- Nurses are concerned to inform me about treatment
- The amount of attention paid to me by nurses is adequate
- Staff are concerned to inform my family and friends

The CentraState Medical Center focused on physician-patient communication as a critical factor in satisfaction (Gutter and Marinaro 2002). The challenge was how to translate patient expectations into physician behavior. The solution was "scripting"—prepared responses that correlate with frequently asked patient questions and desired actions from a consumers' perspective. Physicians wrote their scripts as a group effort, which engaged and empowered their participation. The group identified several verbal and nonverbal behaviors that helped reinforce the prepared responses. Scripting provided consistency in the encounters between physicians and patients and gave physicians the language to manage difficult situations. After the implementation of scripting, patient satisfaction in CentraState's ED rose to the 90th percentile.

Many of the nation's EDs are adopting family-centered care models that permit families to accompany patients during treatment. Emergency facilities are now being redesigned to manage the ED's multiple customer segments, such as trauma, urgent care, pediatric emergency, crisis intervention, and chest pain and observation. To improve service, hospitals are creating a strong partnership with the emergency medicine group and building nursing staff loyalty within the ED in a team culture that emphasizes service. More hospitals are paying close attention to patient satisfaction in the emergency department because of its heavy use and strategic importance. Some hospitals are also setting patient satisfaction targets and incentivizing their physician groups and nursing staff with bonuses for higher satisfaction levels. The highest mean score in Press Ganey's emergency department national database, the 90th percentile, is 86.6, while the top "very good" score is 62.6 (Mylod 2001). Crowding, noise, and waiting in the ED take their toll on patient satisfaction. At the other end of the satisfaction spectrum, emergency departments in the lowest percentile are rated poor by almost one in ten patients (8.4 percent).

SERVICE RECOVERY

Healthcare providers are learning the skills and tactics of service recovery—how to recover from a service error. Although unhappy customers may be few in number, hospitals find themselves expending considerable effort to mollify highly dissatisfied patients. The Press Ganey research organization finds the incidence of highly dissatisfying experiences to be very low, perhaps less than 1 percent, in the top 10 percent of hospitals (Malone and Gwozdz 2002a). Even the lowest 10 percent reported only 4 percent of "poor" responses to satisfaction surveys. Service recovery can move at Internet speed using web-supported patient satisfaction programs. At Community Health System, Inc., in Brentwood, Tennessee, which operates 47 hospitals, patient satisfaction surveys filled out by patients are e-mailed within 24 hours to the unit involved, and managers are encouraged to immediately address any perceived problem (Carpenter 2000).

Customer service is a key dimension of healthcare quality. Service mishaps can destroy a patient's experience, and even lead to lawsuits. Customer service consultants predict that healthcare's unhappy consumers will repeat a dissatisfying medical story 20 times, while other industries estimate an average of 9 to 10 times (Leebov 1993). Not surprisingly, unhappy patients are much less likely to recommend the hospital. Only 9 to 10 percent of those who report poor or very poor experiences would recommend the hospital to others, compared to the 93 percent of patients ranking their experiences as very good.

Dissatisfied patients are trying to send a message, if the service provider is listening. Complaints offer the organization—if they act promptly—an opportunity to make things right with their unhappy consumers. A learning organization recognizes that consumer complaints are important data for continuous performance improvement. Key steps in service recovery include (Malone and Gwodz 2002b)

1. awareness to recognize service errors when they occur;
2. acknowledgement of the mistake;
3. the "blameless apology" (e.g., "I'm sorry this situation occurred");
4. active listening to defuse unhappy patients and families; just letting them talk and not "jumping in right away";

5. acting to amend the problem to make a patient feel better, turning a negative situation into a positive experience; and
6. avoiding future mistakes by identifying recurring problems and looking beyond the symptoms to find root causes.

Healthcare providers may be reluctant to apologize, fearing that acknowledging the mistake could open the door to litigation. However, research in the field of consumer satisfaction and service recovery demonstrates that the first thing a dissatisfied customer wants is a sincere apology.

A huge effort in service recovery occurred in Houston, Texas, when a number of facilities in the Texas Medical Center were deluged by tropical storm Allison. Memorial Hermann Hospital and Memorial Hermann Children's were drenched with 40 million gallons of floodwater, drowning electrical systems and forcing the hospitals to close their doors. At the height of the flooding, Memorial Hermann staff were hand bagging dozens of ventilator patients when the hospitals' backup emergency power systems also failed. Patients were transferred to other hospitals, some as far as 100 miles away, usually with Memorial Hermann staff in attendance (Lowe 2001).

Medical staffs from the two hospitals were quickly given privileges at the outlying hospitals so they could continue care for their patients. The hospital mobilized its family liaison counselors to visit patients and families, driving hundreds of miles in the days following the flood and hospital closures. Memorial Hermann staffers continued to stay in touch with patients during the period of hospitalization and after discharge.

EMPLOYEE SATISFACTION = PATIENT SATISFACTION

Major employers are learning a simple truth. "If you're losing employees, you're losing customers," advises Frederick Reichheld, author of *The Loyalty Effect: The Hidden Force Behind Growth, Profits, and Lasting Value* (1996).

Quality improvement models are recognizing that staff satisfaction is highly correlated with customer satisfaction and ratings. With a national labor shortage, many hospitals may err by inadequately funding training budgets, underinvesting in technology, and offering hiring bonuses instead of addressing staffing levels or patient care issues that are of higher priority to the nursing staff and employees. Technology consultant Bill Porter (1996) believes that if the company's values match the employee's values, the employee is more likely to perceive the company as a quality organization. Those factors most important to employee satisfaction, like level of pride and respect by management, are closely related to the likelihood that employees would recommend their hospital to others (see Table 8.1).

A growing number of hospitals are testing and hiring for service attitude. Computerized testing services are available from companies such as SkillQuest (offered by People Sciences, Inc.) and TalentPlus. SkillQuest supplies computerized testing that can be customized to reflect organizational or industry standards. TalentPlus assists organizations to hire for talent—attitudes and abilities—on the assumption that skills can be trained. In Minnesota, the award-winning Woodwinds Health Campus had 3,800 applicants for 400 positions upon opening in 2000. Although the Twin Cities is a tight labor market, this application pool enabled HealthEast, Woodwinds' sponsor, to screen new employees for customer orientation and hire only those who ranked high in service attitudes.

RECOGNIZING SERVICE EXCELLENCE
A growing number of organizations and media recognize service excellence in hospitals and healthcare settings.

- *U.S. News & World Report* recognizes "America's Best List" in an annual rating. The 2001 listing included 65 hospitals that provided the best care in 17 specialty care areas, with special honor roll recognition to 16 hospitals that were highly ranked in 6 or more of the specialties.
- Solucient "Top 100" hospitals are an annual ranking based on the analysis of financial, clinical, and satisfaction performance data. Solucient also recognizes the top 100 hospitals in a number of specialty care areas, including heart, cancer, orthopedic surgery, and emergency departments.
- The American Nurses Association has revived its magnet hospital recognition program. Hospitals are rated on dozens of criteria by the American Nurses Credentialing Center to demonstrate their excellence in nursing and patient care. To date, nearly 40 hospitals have been awarded magnet status.
- Sodexho Service Awards are annual awards by Sodexho Health Care Services and *Modern Healthcare* magazine, in categories including values integration, internal service, patient service, and vision.

Table 8.1 What is Related to Employee Satisfaction?

Morale/Satisfaction Factor	Overall Satisfaction	Likelihood to Encourage
Level of pride felt	0.70	0.74
Communication by administration	0.70	0.57
Respect shown by manager/supervisor	0.69	0.45
Manager response style to problems	0.69	0.43
New ideas accepted by manager/supervisor	0.68	0.42
Encouragement to think/act independently	0.67	0.42
Adequacy of supervisor support	0.67	0.44
Practicality of organizational goals	0.65	0.49
Ability to disagree with manager/supervisor	0.65	0.41
Accuracy/fairness of evaluations	0.65	0.42

Source: Kaldenberg, D. O., and B. Regrut. 1999. "Do Satisfied Patients Depend on Satisfied Employees? Or Do Satisfied Employees Depend on Satisfied Patients?" *The Satisfaction Report* [Online article; retrieved 8/3/02.] http://www.pressganey.com/research/resources/satmon/text/bin/55.shtm.

- Foster G. McGaw Prize for community service is an annual award program for hospitals and health systems that recognizes innovation and excellence in community-based initiatives.
- Premier Award for Quality is sponsored by Premier, Inc., a national network of nearly 1,500 hospitals across the United States.
- Quality New Jersey is a state-level, Baldrige-type award to recognize organizations that demonstrate outstanding quality practices and that play a positive role in the New Jersey economy.
- Robert Wood Johnson Pursuing Perfection Project is a $20 million national initiative to promote quality innovations. The successful organizations use the Boston-based Institute for Healthcare Improvement's idealized design model of performance improvement. The first round of 236 applicants is reduced to 12 winners for phase-one planning and development. In the future, this will be narrowed to 6 healthcare organizations that will receive multimillion-dollar grants to become models of quality to dramatically improve patient outcomes.

- AARP Modern Maturity named 15 medical centers that the magazine (circulation 30 million) rated among the best at providing patient-centered care.

STRATEGIC IMPLICATIONS

1. *High-level commitment.* Make customer satisfaction one of the organization's top three priorities, and do not waver in the commitment to put patients first. A symbolic policy statement on service from the board provides the philosophical framework, but the real service message must be transmitted every day by management's actions. Spend time on addressing service issues at every meeting of the senior management team. Make patient satisfaction a leading indicator of the health organization's success. Report patient satisfaction scores to the board, medical staff leadership, and middle management on a monthly basis.

2. *Build a service culture.* Cultivating a patient-centered service culture will take years of sustained investment and commitment. So many service moments of truth will take place without any management supervision. Employees and medical staff must respond to service issues from the heart and the culture of the organization, doing what is right for patients and families. Training, scripting, and reinforcing service values are all part of a successful service culture.

3. *Incentivize high-level service.* Reward departments and service units that achieve 90+ percent ratings for customer satisfaction. If ratings are already over the 90th percentile, reward smaller increments and special messages of satisfaction from patients, physicians, and coworkers in other units. Create internal competition for high-level satisfaction ratings, and reward winners. Help lagging units to identify service barriers and overcome them. Provide positive incentives, from bonus dollars to intangibles like theater tickets, closer parking, and out-of-state conferences. To motivate significant improvements in service ratings, put one-third of management bonuses at risk on a unit-by-unit basis. Give special one-time bonuses to high-performing managers whose units have made real service gains.

CONCLUSION

Customer service is no longer the exclusive province of high-touch, for-profit businesses. Healthcare providers must shift their thinking toward a service imperative mind-set with a renewed commitment to personalizing patient care. High levels of patient satisfaction do not just make for good annual report copy—they translate into a more balanced and nurturing work environment for staff, powerful word-of-mouth marketing, and a stronger bottom line.

REFERENCES

ASCI. 2002. "First Quarter Scores, Industries: Hotels, Hospitals, Motion Pictures." East Lansing, MI: Michigan State University.

Bank, L. 2001. "Greenwich Hospital: Getting to 99." *Satisfaction Monitor* (November/December): 8–9.

Carpenter, D. 2000. "Patient Satisfaction: Fast Fixes for Bad Service." *Hospitals & Health Networks* 74 (3): 16.

Carrato, T. F. 2001. "Customer Service Is One of Our Best Stories." *Plain Talk About TRICARE.* [Online article; retrieved 8/3/02.] http://www.tricare.osd.mil/plaintalk/plain_talk.html.

Dow, R., and S. Cook 1997. *Turned On: Eight Vital Concepts to Energize Your People, Customers and Profits.* New York: HarperBusiness.

Gesell, S. 2000. "America's Emergency Departments: One Million Patients Issue 'Report Card'." *Satisfaction Monitor* (July/August): 1–3.

Gutter, E., and M. Marinaro. 2002. "Words . . . The Most Powerful Drug." *Satisfaction Monitor* (January/February): 1–3.

Herzlinger, R. 1997. *Market-Driven Healthcare.* Cambridge, MA: Harvard Business School Press.

Jackson, C. 2001. "California HMO: Doctor Bonuses Based on Patient Satisfaction." *AMA News* [Online article; retrieved 8/3/02.] http://www.ama-assn.org/sci_pubs/amnews/pick_01/bil10730.htm.

Jones, T. E., and E. Sasser. 1995. "Why Satisfied Customers Defect." *Harvard Business Review* November 1.

Kaldenberg, D. O., and B. Regrut. 1999. "Do Satisfied Patients Depend on Satisfied Employees? Or Do Satisfied Employees Depend on Satisfied Patients?" *The Satisfaction Report* [Online article; retrieved 8/3/02.] http://www.pressganey.com/research/resources/satmon/text/bin/55.shtm.

Keenan, A. M. 2000. "The 15/30 Guarantee." *Satisfaction Monitor* (July/August): 1–2.

Lanser, P. 2001. "HCAB Identifies Need for Service Excellence." *Satisfaction Monitor* (November/December): 4–5.

Larkin, H. 1999. "Satisfaction Pays: Happier Patients Can Bring Fatter Wallets." *AMA News* [Online article; retrieved 8/3/02.] http://www.ama.assn.org/sci-pubs/amnews/pick_99/biz0809.htm.

Leebov, W. 1993. *Effective Complaint Handling in Health Care*. Chicago: American Hospital Publishing.

Lowe, J. 2001. "In the Eye of the Storm: Quality Focus Shows Through." *Satisfaction Monitor* (September/October): 1–3.

Malone, M. 2002. "Satisfaction Measurement: Improving Patient Experiences." Presentation. Scottsdale, Arizona. Feb. 22.

Malone, M., and J. Gwozdz. 2002a. "Best Practices: After the 'Oops,' Part 1." *Satisfaction Monitor* (January/February): 8–9.

———. 2002b. "Best Practices: After the 'Oops,' Part 2." *Satisfaction Monitor* (April): 1–15.

Mannello, T. 2000. "Susquehanna Health System: 1999 Global Customer Service Award Winner." [Online article; retrieved 8/3/02.] http://www.pressganey.com/ research/resources/satmon/text/bin/83.shtm.

Mylod, D. E. 2001. "National Norms: How Do You Compare? (Inpatient Care, Emergency Department)." *Satisfaction Monitor* (September/October): 9.

———. 2002. "National Norms: How Do You Compare? (Ambulatory Care)." *Satisfaction Monitor* (January/February): 10.

Peterson, K. 2002. "NET Satisfaction: Revolutionary Web-Based Education and Performance Support Tool." [Online article; retrieved 8/3/02.] http://www.greystone.net/ netsat_index.html.

Porter, W. A. 1996. *Quest for Loyalty: Building Long-Term Relationships with Technology Customers*. Duluth, Georgia: Porter & Associates.

Press Ganey 1999. "One Million Patients Have Spoken: Who Will Listen?" [Online article; retrieved 8/3/02.] http://www.pressganey.com/research/resources/ satmon/text/ bin/65.shtm.

———. 2002. *The 2001 Press Ganey Client Success Stories*. South Bend, IN: Press Ganey. February 18. 1–21.

Reichheld, F. 1996. *The Loyalty Effect: The Hidden Force Behind Growth, Profits, and Lasting Value*. Cambridge, MA: Harvard Business School Press.

Saint Barnabas Medical Center. 2000. "Saint Barnabas Emergency Department Ranks High in National Patient Satisfaction." [Online article; retrieved 8/2/02.] http://www.sbhcs.com/hospitals/saint_barnabas/press/survey.html.

Siskron, F. T. 2002. "It's Time To Make a Decision on Open Access." 75th MDG, Hill Air Force Base, U.S. Air Force. *Skunktales* 1–4

Wood, S. D. 1996. "Member Loyalty: Moving Beyond Satisfaction." *Health Care Systems Economics Report* 1 (4). [Online article; retrieved 8/3/02.] http://www.bayermhc.com/rces/member_loyalty.shtml.

Chapter 9

Competing by Design: Hospitals of the Future Offer Healing Environments

The lesson for all healthcare organizations is clear: provide a built environment that is welcoming to patients, improves their quality of life, and supports families and employees—or suffer the economic consequences in a competitive environment. In addition to attracting patients, the built environment can be a major factor in recruiting and retaining talented staff, increasing philanthropy, community, and corporate support, and enhancing operational efficiency and productivity.

—*Blair Sadler (2001)*

IF YOU THINK of a hospital as an antiseptic environment with harsh lighting, stiff furniture, and views of acoustical tile ceilings from a drab sickbed, think again (Mack 2000). A fresh wave of health facilities promises to reinvent the concept of a hospital and revive the spirit of hospitality in patient care settings. Healthcare architects and designers are updating and upgrading hospitals, with innovative new facilities like Bronson Methodist Hospital in Kalamazoo, Michigan; Doernbecher Children's Hospital in Portland, Oregon; Woodwinds Health Campus in Woodbury, Minnesota; Griffin Hospital in Derby, Connecticut; and Children's Hospital and Health Center in San Diego, California. The emphasis on healing design in these new facilities is long-overdue recognition by the health field that patients' surroundings affect their well-being.

Healthcare architects, space planners, interior designers, and progressive industry suppliers are developing innovative concepts for health facilities, including the following:

- Natural light that penetrates interiors
- Interior open space in atriums, walkways
- Noise reduction and elimination of overhead paging
- Patient privacy and control of the environment

- Healing gardens
- Therapeutic art and sculptures
- Private (one-patient), over-sized rooms
- Hidden storage of supplies and equipment
- Views of the natural environment
- Village-like campuses of ambulatory inpatient facilities
- Integrated physician offices
- Environmentally friendly design
- Cafes, bookstores, and health-related retail shops
- Wellness, fitness, and complementary medicine
- Digital and wireless telecommunications
- Internet access for health-seeking consumers

The best of these new facilities use evidence-based design. Like evidence-based medicine, the goal is to translate research findings on the impact of the built environment on patients' physical and psychological health status into actual operation. More than 125 research projects have been conducted in the United States and around the world testing the healthcare designer's palette of color, light, noise control, art, privacy, space, and scale. The goal of research in healing design is to create health facilities that reduce patient stress, use fewer strong medications, and promote rapid recovery.

HEALING ENVIRONMENTS PLEASE PATIENTS, PROMOTE HEALING

Healing environments aim to create spaces for patient care that engender feelings of peace, hope, joy, reflection, and solace. The potential of pleasant, user-friendly facilities to attract patients and improve their healthcare satisfaction also has been promoted as a marketing strategy (Egger 1999). But the concept of healing environments goes further, to positively affect patients' moods, stress levels, and overall perceptions of health.

Market forces have combined with a growing body of research that shows that physical comfort, and especially connection to the natural world, aid healing by reducing stress. Designer Jain Malkin notes that "Looking at a fireplace or an aquarium can bring down blood pressure. Seeing the sky or feeling the sun on your skin can literally make you feel better . . . It's a long-overdue acknowledgment by the medical community that our surroundings affect our well-being" (Mack 2000).

Healing environments optimize the surroundings of patient care, not just with patient-pleasing design, but also with supportive social systems such as family-centered care, the informed patient, and alternative medicine options. The goal of a healing environment is to transform the hospital or health facility into a place that addresses the human spirit and supports patients and their families to positively cope with and transcend illness.

Researchers are developing a new understanding of how the built environment affects patients. Studies are testing the way in which healthcare surroundings interrelate with medical care, illness, and patient attributes. This field of environmental psychology is called psychoneuroimmunology, focusing on the correlation between stress and health (Gappell 1991). Studies demonstrate that the mind, brain, and nervous system can be directly influenced, positively or negatively, by sensory elements in the environment. The research surprised many designers. Normal consciousness can be maintained only in a constantly changing environment. Therefore, healthcare interiors must be stimulating, not neutral. The drab interiors and unchanging artificial light that are typical of many hospital units may not only dull the senses, but be visually trying and emotionally stressful as well.

According to Rubin, Owens, and Golden (1998), the environment can influence patient outcomes in three primary ways.

1 *Medical care.* The designed environment can support or hinder caregiver actions and medical interventions, making it easier (or harder) for clinicians to do their jobs and facilitating helpful (or harmful) effects. For example, carpeting reduces the stressful noise of healthcare personnel going about their business in the patient's room.
2 *Health status.* The designed environment may strengthen or impair patients' health status and personal characteristics by alleviating (or exacerbating) existing conditions and patients' personal strengths. For example, loss of sleep because of noise in the postoperative setting may prolong recovery time.
3 *Causes of illness.* The designed environment can protect patients from or expose them to causes of illness. For example, the circulation of ultraclean air may protect hospitalized patients from debilitating or even fatal nosocomial infections.

RESEARCH LESSONS ON BUILT ENVIRONMENTS AND PATIENT CARE

Research on the impact of the built environment on patients has linked poor design to negative outcomes such as anxiety, delirium, elevated blood pressure, and increased use of pain drugs (Ulrich 1995). A landmark study in the early 1980s found that 23 postsurgical patients in rooms with views of a stand of trees stayed for fewer postoperative days, received fewer negative evaluative comments in nurses' notes, and required fewer potent analgesics than 23 matched patients in similar rooms with windows facing a brick wall (Ulrich 1984). Dozens of other studies have sought to evaluate the health impacts of factors such as room size and scale, privacy, environmental control by the patient, lighting, color of walls and furnishings, patterns in walls and fabrics, air and ventilation, art, music, windows and views, and relationship with nature.

In 1998, researchers at the Johns Hopkins University prepared a comprehensive review of 84 studies involving the impact of the healthcare environment on patient outcomes. The Center for Health Design in Lafayette, California, sponsored this meta-analysis of research on healing design (Rubin, Owens, and Golden 1998). Hopkins researchers scanned nearly 80,000 articles in the National Library of Medicine to identify a body of research that demonstrated one or more impacts of the built environment on patient outcomes and satisfaction. Although results from these early studies are promising, the Hopkins scientists cautioned that the body of evaluated research on healthcare design is limited and that it is difficult to isolate and change only one feature of a healthcare environment while controlling for all other factors.

EXEMPLARY DESIGNS ADDRESS KEY ISSUES IN PATIENT CARE

Annual healthcare design competitions showcase innovative designs and exemplary facilities. But what really works in terms of patient satisfaction, costs of care, and health impacts? After two decades of research by environmental psychologists, healthcare architects, designers, suppliers, and provider organizations, an understanding is emerging of what works in healing design. The key strategy of the designers is to reduce stress. Healing environments work principally by reducing external sources of stress for patients, such as noise from overhead paging in the hallway, and promoting feelings of control over the environment by the patient, such as personal televisions and music systems.

Other aspects of the built environment can also work to reduce stress, such as giving patients views of nature, providing in-room sleeping accommodations for family members, and allowing access to healing gardens that provide a refuge from the stress of illness and the noise of a hospital environment. Designers are responding with larger rooms and better layouts, repositioning closets, providing wheelchair storage in bedroom closets, hiding high-tech equipment, increasing the amount of natural lighting, redesigning bathrooms, and making family visiting areas more homelike (Varni et al. 2001).

The Woodwinds Health Campus (2000) in Woodbury, Minnesota, is an exemplary health facility that demonstrates the potential of healing design. The Woodwind's stated goal is "to be the innovative, unique, and preferred resource for health, by fundamentally creating the healthcare experience in a way that has not been done before." The project is a joint venture of the HealthEast Care System and Children's Hospitals and Clinics. It looks and feels like a lodge, with stone, wood, and a huge fireplace in the central lobby. When the Woodwinds began recruiting to fill 400 positions to open its new 70-bed facility, they received applications from over 3,800 nurses and healthcare workers. The Woodwinds screens potential hires for their attitudes toward patients and service and conducts extensive training on the Woodwinds' patient-centered philosophy and practices. Julie Schmidt, CHE (2000), the Woodwinds chief executive officer, describes the hospital-employee "partnership that is based on trust, respect, personal and professional integrity, and a constant willingness to work together to serve our customers."

Key components of healing design must address those issues discussed in the following paragraphs (Ulrich 1995).

Psychologically Supportive Environments

Focusing on the concept of stress, the theory of psychologically supportive environments emphasizes that health facilities should be designed to foster coping with stress. In patient care settings, stress can come from a variety of sources. In an episode of illness, many patients experience uncertainty, pain, loss of control, and fears of disability or even death. In healthcare settings, some aspects of the physical facility as well as the processes of care often cause patients to experience negative psychological, physiological, and behavioral manifestations that work against wellness.

From a psychological standpoint, stress can be manifested in a sense of helplessness or feelings of anxiety and depression. Physiologically, stress causes changes in bodily systems, such as increased blood pressure, higher muscle tension, and high levels of circulating stress hormones. Behavioral effects of stress can include verbal outbursts, social withdrawal, passivity, sleeplessness, alcohol or drug abuse, and noncompliance with medication orders.

Psychologically supportive environments bring care closer at the moment of stress. Working with elements of design in the Woodwinds setting, designers use sources of natural light to open up a room or view. Elements like colors and "zero" noise are also designed to help reduce stress.

Sense of Control

The concept of control is well known to designers. Research on employees and workplaces and hospitalized patients has demonstrated that a sense of control is important for feelings of self-esteem and security. Lack of control may result in negative behaviors such as depression, passivity, elevated blood pressure, and reduced immune function. The more a person has a sense of control over the environment, the easier it is to manage the negative effects of a source of stress. Illness confronts patients with a number of problems, such as chronic pain, reduced physical capabilities, loss of independence, or restrictive diets.

Hospital environments can contribute to a loss of control through unfamiliar, noisy, and crowded facilities or confusing wayfinding. A patient's stress levels may be raised if staff is perceived as impersonal, rude, uncaring, or slow to respond to requests for assistance. Anyone who has waited in a hospital emergency room crowded with patients and noisy children, not knowing when they will be seen by a doctor, with a television blaring in the corner and pages interrupting constantly, has certainly experienced the stress of loss of control in a healthcare setting.

Social Support

Healing environments provide space and structure for social interaction. Environmental psychologists have researched healthcare and workplace situations, finding that individuals with a high level of social support experience less stress and have higher levels of wellness. People with lower levels of social support experience both higher rates of illness and less favorable recovery indicators. For example, cardiac patients with higher social support recover more quickly from heart attacks and have more favorable long-term survival rates.

Social interaction in health facilities can be influenced by furniture placement and floor/room layouts. Heavy or unmovable furniture inhibits social interactions, while comfortable, movable furniture that can be arranged in small flexible groups facilitates social interaction (Sommer and Ross 1958, Holohan 1972). Healthcare designers and space planners are initiating layouts that increase social support, such as creating multiple family waiting areas and moving them closer to patient rooms. The Woodwinds Health Campus includes fireplaces in several waiting areas, and some Planetree hospitals have redesigned nursing units to include family social areas with small kitchens.

Positive Distractions

Healthcare designers are learning that positive distractions that provide a moderate level of constructive stimulation can foster a sense of engagement and well-being. A positive distraction can be any environmental feature that elicits positive feelings and holds attention and interest without taxing or stressing the individual.

Lack of positive stimulation can be numbing and depressing for patients. In a moving story, *Bed Number Ten*, a victim of Guillain-Barre syndrome chronicled her despair while she was helpless in a hospital bed for months, staring at the wall or ceiling tiles (Baier and Schomaker 1986). Research in environmental psychology finds several sources of positive distractions such as happy, laughing faces; pets or unthreatening animals; and nature elements such as trees, plants, and views of natural landscapes. The use of nature to aid healing has a long history, back to early Rome and Greece, and Hippocrates' practice under the Plane tree. Roger Ulrich, Ph.D., of the Center for Health Systems and Design at Texas A&M University, has conducted research studies that demonstrate that incorporating natural content and configurations into healthcare design has a beneficial effect on reducing stress and restoring well-being (Ulrich et al. 1991).

Reduced Negative Distractions

Environmental elements can also increase stress if their presence is difficult to ignore. Negative distractions may be built into the environment or are part of processes not under the patient's control. A patient who is awakened by the hospital paging system or has sleep disturbed by employees talking in the hallway when the patient cannot close the door is likely to experience unwarranted stress.

Healthcare patients often must cope with sources of negative distractions. Waiting in a crowded lobby, sitting in stiff, unmovable chairs while a television blares with no control over programming or sound levels certainly constitutes a stressful environment. Designers are introducing layouts, furnishings, and processes that reduce negative distractions and, ideally, replace them with positive distractions.

HEALING GARDENS EXTEND THE CONCEPT OF HEALING DESIGN

Hospitals are reviving an old design concept—healing gardens. As early as the Middle Ages, hospitals within monasteries were built around a garden cloister. Organizing patient rooms around a courtyard filled with sunlight and trees is a more modern version of the garden-centered plan. Unfortunately, many of today's hospitals have lost their touch with nature. Discovery of the germ theory of disease in the nineteenth century reoriented the core concept of the hospital from homelike respite care to a sterile, scientific laboratory. High-tech hospitals with their antiseptic surgeries, elevators, and artificial lighting separate patients from natural surroundings. Air-conditioned, high-rise towers place patients far above the natural environment, while on ground-floor levels, competition for space often leaves many units without windows.

Interest in healing gardens is growing rapidly. Landscape architects and designers are installing gardens and cloister-like spaces in new hospitals and remodeled facilities across the nation. Some gardens emphasize meditation, while others simply offer a shady bench or small pool surrounded by greenery.

In San Diego, the Leichtag Family Healing Garden at Children's Hospital was built to reduce stress, restore hope and energy, and increase consumer satisfaction. The 40 foot by 100 foot garden is located in the middle of the hospital campus and includes Sam the dinosaur, a metal sculpture, as well as a seahorse fountain and 14-foot-tall windmill.

A recent postoccupancy evaluation found that the garden was perceived as a place of restoration and healing, and 50 percent reported that the garden definitely increased their satisfaction and willingness to recommend Children's Hospital (Whitehouse et al. 2001). A majority of consumers (54 percent) reported they felt more relaxed and less stressed after spending time in the healing garden. The hospital is now making further improvements recommended by patients and families, including more trees, additional greenery, and more interactive activities for children.

PLANETREE PROJECTS DEMONSTRATE HEALING ENVIRONMENTS

Since its founding in 1978, Planetree has been a pioneering movement to promote patient-centered care and healing design in hospitals and health facilities. Beginning with a consumer health resource center and a 13-bed model unit in the Pacific Medical Center in San Francisco, the customer-first concepts of Planetree have been an innovative model adopted by other healthcare organizations. Today, the Planetree Alliance, based at Griffin Hospital in Derby, Connecticut, consists of more than 35 hospitals and consumer resource centers that rebuilt their facilities and customer service programs based on Planetree principles.

Planetree has been a pioneer in personalizing, humanizing, and demystifying the healthcare experience for patients and their families (Planetree 2001). Planetree's first director, Robin Orr, is now a consultant in patient-centered care. Her work with Harbor Hospital in Baltimore, Maryland, as well as with the U.S. Air Force's 80 health facilities, demonstrates the possibilities for fundamental change in organizational cultures to become patient focused.

The Griffin Hospital has radically reformed its culture and built a new facility based on Planetree principles. Opened in 1999, Griffin's new 160-bed facility has drawn rave reviews from designers and 96 percent satisfaction ratings from patients. In designing its new building, Griffin passed out detailed surveys to patients and ran focus groups. Patients said they wanted rooms that did not look like hospital rooms; double beds in the obstetrics unit so husbands could sleep nearby; big windows and skylights; and large, comfortable lounges where families could gather.

The result is better than imagined, from the time that consumers hear classical music in the parking lot to the smell of muffins baking in the kitchens on nursing units. Every patient is within 15 feet of his or her primary nurse, thanks to a floor layout that decentralizes staffers closer to patient rooms. Patients get an armload of medical literature on their condition to support the Planetree principle of informed consumers, and staff talks frankly with patients and families. Following another Planetree principle, patients read their own medical records and participate in daily case conferences about the management of their care. Griffin Hospital is a positive tribute to Planetree's commitment to patient-centered care delivered in a healing environment.

"PEBBLE PROJECTS" ASSESS THE IMPACTS OF DESIGN

Hospitals like Griffin demonstrate a powerful link between facility design and the built environment, with positive effects on staff morale and patient satisfaction. Some of healthcare's newest and most innovative hospitals are formally evaluating the fiscal, clinical, behavioral, and health status effects of healthcare design. The Center for Health Design believes the effects of these "pebble projects" may ripple across the entire health field (McMorrow 2001). The Center for Health Design, based in Lafayette, California, is recruiting a consortium of hospitals building new health facilities using principles of healing design. Pebble institutions are committed to research and evaluation to see how well their new facilities work in practice, in terms of cost of operation, patient and family satisfaction, staff morale, use of resources (e.g., pharmaceuticals and labor hours), and healthcare outcomes.

Several organizations have joined with the Center for Health Design (2001) in the evaluation program.

- *Bronson Methodist Hospital, Kalamazoo, Michigan* launched a major redevelopment project to create a state-of-the-art, easily accessible healthcare campus that brings together inpatient care, outpatient care, and physician offices in a patient-focused healing environment. Phases I and II of the $181 million project include a new medical office pavilion, an outpatient pavilion, and an inpatient pavilion. Phase III includes renovation of the institution's north campus buildings.
- *Clarian Health Partners, Indianapolis, Indiana* constructed a 56-bed demonstration cardiovascular comprehensive critical care unit at its Methodist Hospital campus. The new unit combines a former critical care unit and a step-down unit into a single nursing unit. Each headwall is critical care ready, enabling the patient to change levels of care within the same patient room. This innovative design addresses a chronic problem in the critical care unit—50 percent of the patient population may be transferred in or out in a single shift. The hospital has two other cardiovascular critical care units slated for redevelopment, providing an opportunity for baseline comparison with before-and-after design.

- *Children's Hospital and Health Center, San Diego, California*, after a decade of building award-winning health facilities and a healing garden, is constructing a new $25 million children's convalescent hospital. San Diego Children's Center for Child Health Outcomes is an active participant in the Boston-based Institute for Health Improvement's quality improvement programs. Children's has developed prototype outcomes measurement instruments that are being shared with other pebble projects.
- *Barbara Ann Karmanos Cancer Institute and Detroit Medical Center, Detroit, Michigan* is engaging in a joint venture with the Detroit Medical Center to create a unique cancer hospital. Two inpatient units have recently been renovated, while others were not, providing an opportunity to compare key performance indicators such as length of stay, employee turnover, and patient satisfaction.

The pebble projects will use a number of nationally standardized evaluation instruments to test the effects on patients, families, physicians, and nurses. Evaluators in each project will share the results of their ongoing studies including comparisons of outcomes, identification of best practices, and continuous improvements in healthcare design.

TOP TEN TRENDS IN HEALTH FACILITIES

After a decade of slow growth, healthcare design and construction is poised to expand substantially. The baby boom will strongly influence this wave of new and remodeled facilities, and the concepts of healing design will become mainstream. Here are ten of the leading trends that will shape this period of expansion.

1. Healthcare Construction Boom Ahead

Spending on healthcare construction, stalled at $17 billion annually in 1999 and 2000, is poised to boom and could climb to $27 billion by 2010 (Croswell 2001b). Demographics and competition are key forces in this growth scenario. A rapid rise in healthcare facilities construction will be driven by the baby boomers and the expansion of the population to 300 million. The declining power of managed care to steer patients also means that consumers have more choice in selecting a health facility.

Hospitals with capital to improve their health facilities are competing by design to attract patients with specialized centers of excellence, hotel-like surroundings, and consumer-pleasing ambience like a Starbucks cafe in the lobby.

An increase in healthcare construction spending is overdue. Hospitals today are facing the need for significant capital investments to replace aging inpatient facilities and expand space for heavily used services like the emergency department, surgery, and ambulatory care. In the 1990s, most hospitals deferred major capital spending projects because of the fiscal impact of managed care and the Balanced Budget Act. The need to upgrade information systems for Y2K also diverted capital from facilities improvements.

The deferral of capital investment in the 1990s is causing many hospitals to experience capacity problems today. Obsolete facilities carry other costs besides lost revenues. Staff productivity, morale, and turnover can be affected, driving up operating expenses. Older facilities are typically less flexible in use (e.g., two-bed semi-private rooms versus single-room units). Inadequate storage, inefficient layouts, and traffic bottlenecks are commonplace and costly in facilities that were constructed more than 20 years ago.

Tomorrow's health facilities are on the drawing boards, but the lag between planning and construction is masking the upturn in capital investment that is coming. Spending on healthcare construction fell by 1.5 percent in 2000, to $17.6 billion, according to a *Modern Healthcare*'s annual construction and design survey. Across the nation, there were fewer but more expensive projects, as health facility construction costs jumped 20 percent. While the number of hospital replacements dropped by 10 percent in 2000, spending on specialty hospitals, especially those for children and women, climbed by 27 percent (Croswell 2001b).

2. Built in Quality

The most innovative, patient-pleasing health facilities are connecting the concepts of healing environments, quality improvement, patient safety, and reduced medical errors. The Institute of Medicine's definition of quality includes characteristics such as equitable, safe, effective, efficient, patient-centered, and timely care. The Center for Health Design is now working with the Institute of Medicine and the Institute of Healthcare Improvement to build facilities that enhance the delivery of quality care.

3. Specialized Facilities

The hospital of the future is being reconceptualized as an upscale shopping center of specialty care facilities. Heart, cancer, and women's services are the most popular centers of excellence, but many hospitals are focusing on other consumer segments and diseases. Cynthia Hayward (2001), a facilities planning consultant, observes that LASIK surgery, high-speed computed tomography heart scanning, breast centers, neuroscience centers, and emergency departments are getting their own facilities, parking, entrances, and exclusive patient amenities.

A strong, well-designed, specialized facility can change a local hospital into a regional or a national competitor. In southern California, Hoag Memorial Hospital Presbyterian's award-winning remodel of its breast care and imaging center features an environment that is consumer-pleasing and serene (Takahama 2000). To overcome its underground location, designers used recessed lighting, translucent glass, and a lowered ceiling to create an impression of light slanting in from outside. The overall feeling of the 8,500-square-foot facility is a spa, with golden-toned pear wood, black steel, and wood beams on sand-colored carpet, reflecting the hospital's location on the Pacific Ocean. Patient dressing rooms have been expanded, museum-quality art work now hangs on the walls, and fluffy white cotton bathrobes have replaced the hospital's flimsy paper gowns.

4. "Green" Design

Interest in environmentally friendly "green" design is rising. At Chicago's 2001 NeoCon exposition for interior design and facilities management, a number of the more than 1,200 exhibitors showcased furnishings, lighting, fabrics, and equipment that incorporated natural elements into facilities and interiors (Mannino 2001). Green designers use skylights, windows, and atriums to flood interiors with light. Healing environments are built with stone, wood, and other natural materials. Waterfalls, streams, and pools create parklike or garden settings, both inside and outside health facilities.

5. Innovative Technology

Healing design is also techno-friendly. Patient-centered environments apply technology in innovative ways to reduce sources of negative stress on patients and optimize their sense of control, privacy, and well-being. At the new Doernbecher Children's Hospital at the University of Oregon Health Sciences Center, patients can align their window shades from bed-level electronic controls to brighten or darken the room, as well as control their in-room audio-visual system for television and music with a remote device at bedside.

Other future-minded facilities like HealthEast's Woodwinds Health Campus are proactively using technology to enhance the patient experience. In the Woodwinds, a wireless paging system eliminates pages while bedside computer terminals allow nursing staff and doctors to plug in portable electronic medical records (Howatt 2000). The Woodwinds' staffers are remotely monitored using a radio system and computer chips imbedded in every employee identification badge. The hospital describes itself as "paper-lite" and plans to be paperless in the future.

6. Baby Boomer Consumers

Baby boomer women are the target customers of the healing design movement. More than 40 million women between ages 35 and 55 fall in America's largest generation, born between 1946 and 1964. They are the most frequent "health seekers" on the Internet, according to the Pew Internet and American Life ongoing study (Fox and Rainie 2000). Many baby boomers were influenced by the age of Aquarius and its orientation toward spirituality, eastern religious philosophies, and feminism. They are very accepting of alternative and complementary medicine and are attracted to healthcare providers with a wellness orientation.

Baby boomers were also branded the "me" generation in the 1980s for their egoism and demanding "have it now" attitude. Still fussy and self-centered, this generation now dominates finance, politics, management hierarchies, and consumer markets. Baby boomers are the target customers for specialized facility development projects that incorporate patient-centered care and healing environment features. Boomers have significant discretionary income and are armed with Internet information on the latest treatments, from cancer care to knee replacement. "Boomers are discovering they can get a plane ticket to a world-class health facility in another city for the cost of a good dinner," Cynthia Hayward (2001) notes. "Patients are thinking globally and acting globally."

7. Health and Spirituality

The connection between health, well-being, and spirituality is being discovered by the medical community. A spiritual orientation is natural in religious-sponsored hospitals but, beyond chapels and chaplains, is somewhat less common in nonreligious health facilities. Architects and designers are incorporating the desire for spiritual support and meditation into their floor plans and healing gardens. Mid-Columbia Medical Center, a Planetree hospital in The Dalles, Oregon, recently constructed a labyrinth for walking and meditation modeled on the walkway at the cathedral in Chartres, France. The hospital has sponsored conferences on healing and spirituality and has a center for wellness and alternative medicine.

8. Modular Design

The hospital room of the future may be a module that can be installed in an existing or new facility. Wellness, LLC, has designed the wellness room as a packaged module (*Business Wire* 1999).

The innovative concept—introduced at the Symposium on Health-care Design in Boca Raton, Florida—features room designs that promote healing, increase patient satisfaction, and improve staff efficiency. Wellness rooms are a complete package that includes lighting, walls with built-in wiring and mechanicals, vinyl finishes, furnishings, an Americans with Disabilities Act–compliant patient bathroom, and an in-room nursing station. Healing environment concepts like color, nature, and control over the environment have been built into the modules, and wellness rooms feature soothing colors and curved surfaces. Easy-to-clean materials have been installed and sharp corners have been eliminated to simplify cleaning. The rooms can be installed in half the time of conventional construction and can be leased or purchased.

9. Art and Music

Nontraditional elements mix with architecture and interior design to create healing environments where art helps overcome the sterile nature of some health facilities. Pieces of sculpture mark major corridors or entrances to units to aid in wayfinding. Although art and music can be positive stress-relievers, Helen Orem (1992), art director for the Clinical Center of the National Institutes of Health (NIH), cautions that they can also be a major source of stress if not done well. Research shows that patients generally prefer art with representational, natural content, such as scenes of nature or a vase of flowers. Abstract art can inspire overt negative reactions; in fact, in one instance some abstract pieces were so disturbing they were attacked and destroyed on a psychiatric ward (Ulrich 1986).

In the outpatient center at the NIH Clinical Center, a sculpture called Healing Waters was selected for the lobby as a statement piece—a strong visual element that defines the purpose and character of the place without words (Orem 1992). In the selection of art for health facilities, designers must walk a fine line between stimulating and soothing without being bland. At the NIH Clinical Center, designers transformed a long corridor in a postsurgical unit into a walkway that encourages patients to exercise by moving from one painting or print to the next, with descriptions telling something about the artist, as well as noting how many post-recovery feet the patient has walked from piece to piece.

Music is also being introduced in health facilities. Inspired by the popularity of the Nordstrom's grand piano in many stores, innovative hospitals such as Mid-Columbia Medical Center and the Woodwinds Health Campus are placing pianos in their lobbies with live music for patients in the afternoons. Personal audio-visual systems in patient rooms also include pillow speakers so patients can listen to music of their choice.

10. Healthcare Architecture/Design Specialty

The field of healthcare architecture and design is becoming increasingly specialized. A new organization, the American College of Healthcare Architects (ACHA), was recently established to certify the field's most respected architecture professionals. ACHA is the first organization to provide certification in a specialized field of architecture, according to its president Kirk Hamilton (Croswell 2001a). As of January 2001, some 185 architects successfully completed ACHA certification, and 4,000 architects working in healthcare were invited to participate in that year's examination. Certification requires five years of practice in the United States, a minimum of three years in the healthcare specialty, submission of a portfolio of healthcare projects, and successful completion of ACHA's national examination.

STRATEGIC IMPLICATIONS FOR HOSPITALS, PHYSICIANS, AND HEALTH PLANS

1. *Employ healing design in new facilities.* Use research findings on healing design to create exemplary inpatient and ambulatory facilities. A new facility sends a message about values, priorities, and patient-centered philosophy. A building based on healing design principles can be a great resource to raise patient and staff satisfaction levels. An extraordinary building can be a magnet for patient self-referral and staff recruitment. Participate in evaluation programs like the pebble projects to evaluate the benefits and impacts of design on new buildings and retrofitted spaces.

2. *Retrofit and remodel.* Bring older facilities into the twenty-first century by remodeling and retrofitting with healing design principles. Incorporate natural light and views of nature into building

interiors. Add representational art in hallways and public spaces. Use wireless telecommunications and carpeting to reduce noise. Look for opportunities to build healing gardens in spaces between buildings.

3. *Take healing design into the community.* Look for opportunities to take healing design concepts outside the hospital setting. Work with schools and students to build gardens. Assist nursing homes to retrofit their facilities with art, color, and healing gardens. Collaborate to bring healing design concepts into the community with local elected officials and public agencies, such as public housing, public health, and parks and recreation.

CONCLUSION

The concept of healing design will not gain widespread acceptance until a solid business case provides evidence that exemplary design of health facilities pays off in terms of increased volume, higher patient satisfaction, lower staff turnover, and positive health effects. Advocates of healing design believe that facilities designed to be patient centered and therapeutic will be magnets for consumers. Baby boomers respond very positively to facilities like Griffin Hospital, Northwestern Memorial Hospital, and the Woodwinds Health Campus. These exemplary facilities offer greater privacy, views of nature, and innovative education programs and communication systems. These generate higher patient satisfaction, market ratings, and revenues as patients drive past conventional hospitals to get to these award-winning facilities.

At Bronson Methodist Hospital, chief executive officer Frank Sardone (2002) reports that in only one year after opening their $180 million replacement hospital, the patient-centered facility and healing garden have raised patient volumes in orthopedic surgery, neurosurgery, and cardiac care, while boosting market share by five points.

On the other side of the balance sheet, healing design may reduce expenses and lead to cost reductions such as the following:

- Shorter lengths of stay
- Lower costs per case
- Reduced use of stronger drugs
- Fewer negative notes in nursing progress reports
- Reduced nurse hours per patient
- Improved staff morale
- Reduced turnover and costs for recruitment

The bottom line is happier patients who use fewer strong medications, are easier to care for, go home sooner, love their hospital, and recommend it to others. In 1991, architect Derek Parker estimated the cost savings—shorter stays, drug savings, and labor costs—from a "better building" to be $10 million a year for a 300-bed hospital (Parker 1991). Parker's 1991 estimate would be $15 to $20 million in today's dollars.

Tangible proof in dollars and cents exists to convince skeptical executives and boards that healing design is a winning strategy to reap ample return on investment. In San Diego, the Children's Hospital and Health Center is making the business case for healing design and patient satisfaction. Since launching a campuswide building program a decade ago, Children's innovative hospital facilities and healing gardens have been a major success with patients, with satisfaction scores and market share rising more than ten points. At the same time, the hospital has increased its annual philanthropy over the ten-year period, from $4 million to over $16 million in community giving. CEO Blair Sadler (2001) is a champion for healing design, seeing the payoff in higher volumes from the investment in family-centered facilities.

REFERENCES

Baier, S., and M. Z. Schomaker. 1986. *Bed Number Ten*. Boca Raton, FL: CRC Press.

Business Wire. 1999. "Patient Room of the Future: A Healing Environment Focused on Patient-Centered Care and Staff Efficiency." *Business Wire* August 30.

Center for Health Design. 2001. "Creating a Proposed Partnership Between the Center for Health Design and Leading Innovative Healthcare Organizations." *Healthcare Design* 1 (1): 5–6.

Croswell, C. L. 2001a. "Reputations Have New Foundation." *Modern Healthcare* 31 (11): 36.

———. 2001b. "Building New Strategies: Construction Firms Coping with Array of Fiscal and Corporate Challenges." *Modern Healthcare* 31 (11): 23–36.

Egger, E. 1999. "Designing Facilities to Be Patient-Focused." *Health Care Strategic Management* 17: 19–22.

Fox, S., and L. Rainie. 2000. "The Online Health Care Revolution: How the Web Helps Americans Take Better Care of Themselves." Pew Internet & American Life Project, November 26. 1–23. Washington, DC: Pew Foundation

Gappell, M. 1991. "Psychoneuroimmunology." In *Innovations in Healthcare Design*, 115–19, edited by S. O. Marberry. New York: Van Nostrand Reinhold

Hayward, C. 2001. Author interview. August 2.

Holohan, C. J. 1972. "Seating Patterns and Patient Behavior in an Experimental Day-room." *Journal of Abnormal Psychology* 80: 115–24.

Howatt, G. 2000. "New Hospital Takes Unconventional Route: Woodwinds Hospital in Woodbury Will Incorporate Technology and a Holistic Philosophy." *Minneapolis Star Tribune* March 9.

Mack, L. 2000. "Commentary." *Minneapolis Star Tribune* July 30.

Mannino, J. 2001. "Thousands of Product Introductions for Commercial and Residential Design Shown at NeoCon World's Trade Fair." PR *Newswire* June 18.

McMorrow, E. 2001. "Have a Pebble Project?" *Facilities Design & Management* (March): 2.

Orem, H. G. 1992. "Art for Health: Emerging Trends." In *Innovations in Healthcare Design*, 162–176, edited by S. O. Marberry. New York: Van Nostrand Reinhold

Parker, D. 1991. "A Better Building's Benefits." *Modern Healthcare* 21 (47): 30.

Planetree. 2001. "Mission of Planetree." Derby, CT: Planetree Alliance, 1–8.

Rubin, H. R., A. J. Owens, and G. Golden. 1998. "An Investigation to Determine Whether the Built Environment Affects Patients' Medical Outcomes." Martinez, CA: Center for Health Design

Sadler, B. 2001. "Design to Compete in Managed Healthcare." *Facilities Design & Management* (March): 1–4.

Sardone, F. 2002. "Outcomes from Our First Year in *The New Bronson*." Presentation to the Pebble Partner Colloquium, Scottsdale, AZ February 21.

Schmidt, J. 2000. Introductory letter to potential employees. Recruitment packet. Woodbury, MN: The Woodwinds Heath Campus.

Sommer, R., and H. Ross. 1958. "Social Interaction on a Geriatrics Ward." *International Journal of Social Psychiatry* 4: 128–33.

Takahama, V. 2000. "A Design for Healing: Architect Puts Her Experiences into Designing Breast-Care Centers." *The Orange County Register* August 28.

Ulrich, R. 1984. "View Through a Window May Influence Recovery From Surgery." *Science* 224: 420–21.

———. 1986. *Effects of Hospital Environment on Patient Well-Being*. Department of Psychiatry and Behavioral Medicine, Research Report Series 9. Trondheim, Norway: University of Trondheim.

———. 1995. "Effects of Healthcare Interior Design on Wellness: Theory and Recent Scientific Research." In *Innovations in Healthcare Design*, edited by S. O. Marberry, 88–104. New York: Van Nostrand Reinhold.

Ulrich, R. et al. 1991. "Stress Recovery During Exposure to Natural and Urban Environments." *Journal of Environmental Psychology* 11: 201–30.

Varni, J. W. et al. 2001. "An Evaluation of the Built Environment at Children's Convalescent Hospital, San Diego." Unpublished article. San Diego, CA: Center for Child Health Outcomes, Children's Hospital & Health Center.

Whitehouse, S. et al. 2001. "Evaluating a Children's Hospital Garden Environment: Utilization and Consumer Satisfaction." *Journal of Environmental Psychology* 21 (8): 1–14.

Woodwinds Health Campus. 2000. "Living the Vision: How the Woodwinds Guiding Principles Are Transforming the Health Care Experience." Woodbury, MN: The Woodwinds Health Campus.

Chapter 10

Culture of Excellence

We are what we repeatedly do. Excellence, therefore, is not an act, but a habit.

—*Aristotle*

NEARLY ALL HEALTHCARE organizations aspire to high quality in the services they provide. Healthcare organizations' mission and vision statements commonly refer to the quality of the services they offer or aspire to provide. Some organizations also tout other aspects of their purported excellence as described in preceding chapters of this book: service, caring environment, facilities, technology, physicians, and other professional staff. The reality, however, is that few healthcare organizations are clearly distinguished in the markets in which they compete, and even for those that are, their positions are rarely established in a clear-cut manner, communicated effectively, or embedded in the culture of the organization and readily sustainable.

Although most healthcare organizations have at least some pockets of excellence, these tend to be the exception rather than the norm and are rarely used for competitive advantage. Competition in recent years in healthcare has been dominated by the related themes of horizontal integration and vertical integration. In both cases, integration represents an attempt to gain a stronger market position through size advantages rather than quality. Although some competitive advantage may be gained through integration, the healthcare experience is similar to that outside of healthcare, and, in fact, neither horizontal nor vertical integration has proven to be an effective competitive strategy.

LOOKING BEYOND HEALTHCARE

Compare the healthcare experience to that of leading service companies outside of healthcare. Two in particular—Federal Express and Starbucks Coffee—provide excellent examples.

Federal Express

The Federal Express Corporation (FedEx) revolutionized the mail and package delivery industry over the past 30 years. FedEx has emphasized creating transportation, information, and logistics networks to provide true customer value. Although it transports millions of packages each day, its lost-package rate is extremely low, and its advantage derives from the extremely high reliability of its services. As a result, numerous cases have been reported in which FedEx has been used in large companies to transport packages from one floor in a building to another, effectively replacing (free) interoffice mail.

FedEx has raised the bar continuously and revolutionized the overnight package delivery industry through innovations such as real-time management of vehicles, people, packages, routes, and weather conditions. As its competitors have mimicked its advances, FedEx has stayed a step or two ahead with further innovations and even greater reliability with systems that continually seek to make customer-related activities more accessible and easy to use. Its efforts were recognized when the $22 billion company won the first Malcom Baldrige National Quality Award for service in 1990. Numerous other accolades have followed including being ranked tenth on the 2003 *Fortune* list of most admired global companies and eighth on the 2003 *Fortune* list of most admired companies in the United States (FedEx Corporation 2003).

Starbucks Coffee

Another industry maverick, Starbucks Coffee Company, created and continues to dominate the high-end coffee bar industry, while pursuing its objective of being the most recognized and respected brand in the world. The company has more than 4,700 stores worldwide and posted consolidated net revenues of $2.4 billion in 2000 (HP Services 2000).

Starbucks took a stale commodity, coffee, and gave it a fresh image, allowing it to charge two to three times the then-going price for a cup of coffee. Starbucks developed the consumers' appetite for exceptional rather than ordinary coffee, thus allowing it to obtain a premium price for its product. It coupled this distinctive product with a pleasant and relaxed atmosphere in its stores and has attempted to make its product highly accessible to the public through many distribution points in the areas in which it operates and extended hours of operation in each store.

Like Federal Express, Starbucks has attracted a host of imitators but has stayed ahead of the competition with continued product enhancements and a consistently high level of service that have established the firm as the premier purveyor of coffee in the world and earned recognition for the company through numerous service, quality, and ethics awards for its humanitarian activities and corporate leadership with environmental issues. Starbucks received the "Excellence in Alliances" award in 2002 from the Association of Strategic Alliance Professionals and has consistently been named by *Business Ethics Magazine* as one of "The 100 Best Corporate Citizens" (Starbucks.com 2003).

WHAT MAKES A COMPANY EXCEPTIONAL?

What differentiates the exceptional companies from the rest of the pack? All operate in highly competitive industries and realize their positions in the market are fragile, subject to constant and creative competitor attacks.

First, most industries are much more dynamic than healthcare, and competition is carried out in a far more sophisticated and continuous manner. Unlike healthcare, there is explicit recognition that competition is a daily—if not a minute-by-minute—affair, and today's success is no guarantee of even tomorrow's viability.

Second, exceptional companies thoroughly understand the nature of the markets in which they operate and how to obtain competitive advantage in these markets. They clearly understand the value of differentiation—not just to be different, but to be different and better in ways that their customers value greatly. And the exceptional companies continually strive to improve, encouraging ongoing innovation to meet customers' future needs. These companies foster entrepreneurship *and* intrapreneurship, with a steady stream of advances. Although not all of these advances make it to the market and succeed, those that do create new distance between the company and its competitors.

Third, and maybe most important, the exceptional companies foster a culture that demands excellence. Being second, average, or even above average—but not the best—is not acceptable. Inherent in these organizations, at all levels, is a constant striving for excellence. Such a culture attracts employees who want to be associated with a winner and contribute to its success. Change, growth, and continuous improvement are daily realities. Although such a culture would be desirable in any company, the reality is that it is not all that common. It takes exceptional leadership, with an unusual and near-maniacal commitment to excellence, to instill that culture in an organization and then maintain it over time.

LESSONS FOR HEALTHCARE ORGANIZATIONS

What lessons do these exceptional companies offer to healthcare organizations? It is clear that competition in healthcare is escalating, probably far more rapidly than most realize. However, the lack of explicit recognition of the competitive nature of most markets and fairly simplistic competitive analysis and behavior by healthcare providers result in an inability to deliver on the quality promise that nearly all healthcare organizations make in their mission or vision statements.

A fundamental failing is the inability or lack of desire of healthcare leaders to do what it takes to achieve the promise of excellence. Contrast the typical healthcare organization with Federal Express, Starbucks, or any other quality leader. Why don't healthcare organizations approach competition in the same ways as other industries? Although it would be simple to suggest that it is structurally impossible to excel because healthcare delivery is more difficult, or healthcare organizations are more complex, or market conditions are so unusual compared to other industries, such is not the case. What, then, *is* the root cause?

At the opposite end of the spectrum from excellence, healthcare errors have been put in the spotlight by the Institute of Medicine (IOM). In a series of groundbreaking reports, the IOM has dissected the toll—in terms of lives and dollars—that preventable medical errors cost the United States each year. It notes that "the decentralized and fragmented nature of the healthcare delivery system . . . or 'nonsystem'" is a commonly cited contributing factor to the high rate of medical errors, but also that "healthcare is a decade or more behind many other high-risk industries in its attention to ensuring basic safety" (IOM 2000). Further, the IOM cites the lack of leadership at all levels—the government, individual providers, clinicians, and management—to make safety a high priority. Reaching for excellence becomes very difficult when problems are so widespread at such a fundamental level in healthcare.

Healthcare organizations have become increasingly short term in their orientation, and, unlike other large service companies, healthcare organizations are much more reactive than proactive. The quest for excellence requires vision, long-term commitment, and the belief that it is possible to create a very different future for the organization despite huge obstacles along the way. This perspective may be harder for healthcare organizations to adopt than is the case in other industries.

Management

The federal Centers for Medicare & Medicaid Services (CMS) began producing a series of reports on various parts of the healthcare delivery system in 2001. Its report on acute care hospitals examines the differences between those hospitals that perform well financially and those that do not. It quotes Dennis Farrell of Moody's Investor Services, who comments that "one of the key differences between the 'haves' and the 'have-nots' is the quality and depth of senior management" (CMS 2002):

> We used to look at management, and if the same people were there for 20 years we'd say 'Good, stable management team.' If I see somebody who's been there 20 years now . . . I get a little nervous. Do they have the tools and equipment to make the decision they are being faced with today, or are they just some[one] that the rest of the team would like to get rid of?
>
> Today, rating agencies and investors are more likely to look for specific management experience and skills needed to cope with today's market, either in the person of top managers or among individuals they have hired to run their organizations. Experience in managed care, mergers, acquisitions, and network development are highly prized. So are managers capable of operating new ventures.

In his book *Good to Great*, Jim Collins (2001) distinguishes among different levels of capabilities that organizational leaders possess: an *effective* leader "catalyzes commitment to and vigorous pursuit of a clear and compelling vision, stimulating higher performance standards." A *top* leader "builds enduring greatness through a paradoxical blend of personal humility and professional will." These latter leaders "are fanatically driven, infected with an incurable need to produce sustained results. They are resolved to do whatever it takes to make the company great, no matter how big or hard the decisions."

Championship

John Griffith (2000) believes that "stakeholders will put increasing pressure on integrated health systems (IHS) for measured performance, demanding data on quality and patient satisfaction, while simultaneously pressing for lower cost . . . . Quality of care in particular will face increasing scrutiny." He suggests that exemplary healthcare organizations will be considered "champions." "Championship is a combination of the will—leadership and commitment—and the way—systems and procedures. In sports, both the desire to win and the mastery of skills make champions. In managing large corporations, moral commitment and solid systems make champions." Further, he notes that "championship must be dynamic . . . any real IHS must start with the systems they already have and build systematically toward excellence. Champions will reach the limits of current practice; they will invent the best practices of the future" (Griffith 2000).

Entrepreneurship

A related deficiency in healthcare organizations is entrepreneurship. To become a "champion," in Griffith's vernacular, one must embrace and use change as an advantage. As Peter Drucker (1995) has noted, "[e]ntrepreneurs see change as the norm and as healthy. But—and this defines entrepreneur and entrepreneurship—the entrepreneur always searches for change, responds to it, and exploits it as an opportunity."

Entrepreneurs are innovators; "they discover or create an innovation to exploit an opportunity . . . build and grow companies to bring their innovation to market . . . and take significant, calculated, personal risk in building their companies" (National Commission on Entrepreneurship 2001a). The drive for excellence demands this type of perspective in today's increasingly dynamic environment.

One of the myths of entrepreneurship is that it requires a breakthrough invention, usually technological in nature. "Having a breakthrough invention, or a radically new process is not a necessary element . . . far more common are EGCs (entrepreneurial growth companies) like Jiffy Lube, which brought moderate change and certainly marketable distinctions—but not 'revolution'—to the way we change our oil" (National Commission on Entrepreneurship 2001b).

Several well-known growth companies have thrived without early reliance on inventions or proprietary processes. Charles Schwab and other discount brokers found a way to make money with a new pricing strategy that encouraged individual investors to bypass traditional money managers. By guaranteeing the uniformity of the eating experience through tightly controlled franchises, McDonalds and other fast-food restaurants found a powerful way to win market share. Sam Walton improved on the idea of discount retailing—developed by predecessor stores like Ann & Hope—and used careful site selection and rigorous inventory control to help create the Wal-Mart empire (National Commission on Entrepreneurship 2001b).

MEASURING AND MAINTAINING SUCCESS

Griffith and others believe that excellent healthcare organizations will need to measure and demonstrate their performance advantages in the future. Balanced scorecard approaches (Kaplan and Norton 1996), which measure performance in a variety of key dimensions, are becoming increasingly prevalent both outside and now within healthcare. Figure 10.1 presents Griffith's perspective on the critical areas and measures for champion healthcare organizations.

Regardless of whether these or other measures are used, it is no longer sufficient to proclaim "we are a high-quality healthcare organization." Today's and tomorrow's successful organizations must provide concrete indicators of leading performance. As the field advances, it becomes possible and imperative to provide increasingly targeted measures of performance success, including data that clearly demonstrate performance advantages over other competing providers. Such data will provide direct competitive benefits to the best organizations and have the related benefit over time of raising the bar for all healthcare organizations, as few will wish to be considered average or inferior.

And the quest for excellence must be an ongoing one, with continual improvements necessary to maintain advantage over other providers. The ability to measure performance in key areas such as patient satisfaction, outcomes quality, and health status improvement will result in regular review and adjustment of strategy and operations to achieve ever higher levels of performance. Thus performance measurement and modification will be integrated into day-to-day management of healthcare organizations. While management will have principal responsibility for performance measurement and improvement, the board should perform a regular, periodic oversight role to make sure the organization is on track with its drive for excellence and makes the appropriate strategy and operational changes if it is not. This reflects the philosophy of the balanced scorecard approach, which is employed with increasing frequency.

Figure 10.1 Key Areas and Measures for Champion Healthcare Organizations

Organizational Process	Critical Questions	Key Measures
1. Governance and strategic management	◆ What markets do we serve? ◆ What are the priorities of those markets? ◆ What is the total funding level available? ◆ Have we chosen the correct partners?	◆ Outcomes quality ◆ Patient satisfaction ◆ Market share by service ◆ Unit cost ◆ Profitability
2. Clinical quality	◆ Are we achieving optimum outcomes? ◆ Are patients delighted with services? ◆ Are we providing effective prevention	◆ Outcomes measures by disease entity ◆ Patient satisfaction data by sites of care ◆ Measures of preventable diseases and prevention programs
3. Clinical organization	◆ Can we compete for the best caregivers? ◆ Are our caregivers satisfied? ◆ Do we have competitive unit costs for clinical services?	◆ Worker and physician satisfaction ◆ 360-degree review ◆ Recruitment and retention data
4. Financial planning	◆ Can we generate enough capital to remain competitive?	◆ Profit by service line ◆ Forecast of capital requirements ◆ Balance sheet indicators
5. Planning and marketing	◆ Do we have data to support strategic analysis? ◆ Are we investing in the right services and equipment? ◆ Do we have effective communication with our markets?	◆ Governing board and user satisfaction with market data and forecasts ◆ Historic accuracy of forecasts and implemented proposals
6. Information services	◆ Do we have useful data for patient care? ◆ Do we have quantitative data describing our work processes? ◆ Do we have historical data for trend analysis and benchmarks for comparison?	◆ Caregiver satisfaction with online data ◆ Satisfaction of work improvement teams ◆ Ability to produce historical and benchmark information on activities and service lines
7. Human resources	◆ Do we have the right numbers of the right people? ◆ Do we have competitive compensation programs? ◆ Do we have excessive turnover and absenteeism?	◆ Turnover, vacancy, and absenteeism rates ◆ Worker satisfaction with compensation ◆ Costs of benefits and incentive programs
8. Planning and marketing	◆ Do we have the right facilities/locations? ◆ Are our plant costs competitive? ◆ Are plant services satisfactory? ◆ Are supplies costs competitive?	◆ Occupancy of facilities ◆ Costs of plant operations ◆ Costs of supplies ◆ Failure rates and complaints about plant services

Source: Griffith, J. R. "Championship Management for Healthcare Organizations." *Journal of Healthcare Management* 45 (1): 17–30.

In measuring performance and maintaining success, the organization is building toward a culture of excellence where the need to be better than the pack is fundamental and differentiates the organization from the competition. This point is discussed in a series of publications by Jim Collins and Jerry Porras together, and most recently by Collins in his business best seller *Good to Great*. They write,

> [c]ompanies that enjoy enduring success have core values and a core purpose that remain fixed while their business strategies and practices endlessly adapt to a changing world. The dynamic of preserving the core while stimulating progress is the reason that companies such as Hewlett-Packard, 3M, Johnson & Johnson, Procter & Gamble, Merck, Sony, Motorola, and Nordstrom have become elite institutions able to renew themselves and achieve superior long-term performance. (Collins and Porras 1996).

In a similar vein, today's leading authority on corporate and competitive strategy, Michael Porter (1996), says,

> In many companies, leadership has degenerated into orchestrating operational improvements and making deals. But the leader's role is broader and far more important . . . the leader must provide the discipline to decide which industry changes and customer needs the company will respond to, while avoiding organizational distractions and maintaining the company's distinctiveness.

TAKING EXCELLENCE TO THE NEXT LEVEL: LESSONS FOR THE FUTURE

In designing a strategy to compete on excellence, organizations must recognize the stage of market development in which they operate. The five stages of competition presented in Figure 10.2 provide an appropriate point of departure for examining market characteristics. Only a very few healthcare organizations have progressed to the most advanced stage, V, with a few more in stages IV and III. The overwhelming majority of organizations are still mired in stages I and II. Therefore, within the framework, ample room exists for improvement for nearly all healthcare organizations.

However, as the leaders in stage V push the envelope, it is conceivable that additional advanced stages will emerge. It is hard to see where this

Figure 10.2   Five Stages of Competition

Stage	Market Strategy	Physician Strategy	Payer Strategy	Pricing Strategy	Workforce Strategy	Quality Strategy	Management Strategy	Customer Strategy
V. Consumer Driven	Competing on Excellence	Centers of Excellence	Indespensable Provider	Premium	Culture of Excellence	Demonstrably Superior Quality	Visionary Leadership	World-Class Service
IV. Retail Medicine	Niches	Joint Ventures	Selective Contracting	Retail	Pay Above Market	Benchmarking	Pay for Performance	Designed Experiences
III. Consolidated Brand	Market Leverage	Networks	Push-back	Wholesale	Team-Building	Corporate Metrics/IT Systems	Centralized Planning/Budgeting	Mass Market/Customer Relationship Management
II. Vertical Integration	Comprehensive Services	Acquisition	Physician-Hospital Organization	Packaged	Career Ladders	CQI Initiatives	Decentralized Management	One-Stop Shopping
I. Local Franchise	Community Relations	Recruitment	Multi-year Contracts	Discount	Institutional Loyalty	Find-and-Fix Errors	Own the Business	Convenience/Access

Source: Health Strategies & Solutions, Inc., 2003. Used by permission.

may take healthcare now, with so much room for improvement. Undoubtedly, the horizon remains capable of being stretched further, and today's leaders will seek to do that.

What, then, can the typical healthcare organization do to move forward?

- *Get unstuck.* Break out of today's paradigm and recognize that the field is moving from the strategies of the past to those of the future. These strategies will be increasingly consumer driven and reward those organizations that best satisfy consumer needs.
- *Resolve to be a real competitor.* Take off the gloves! Break loose! Learn about advanced competitive strategies inside and outside of the healthcare industry.
- *Lead, don't follow.* As this chapter highlights, strong leadership is critical to success. Although movers and followers may experience some temporary success, long-term advantage will accrue to those who break out of the pack and put more distance between their organizations and the competition.
- *Measure, fine tune, improve.* The drive for advantage is increasingly dependent on demonstrably better performance, which requires measurement of comparative performance and adjustment as required. It also needs to be a regular, ongoing function of management.
- *Develop and maintain sustainable competitive advantage.* Create an organization where excellence is difficult to mimic: core values, ideology, systems, and processes unique to the organization are difficult or impossible to adopt and adapt in competing organizations. Achieving excellence may be the stated target, but doing it in a way that is sustainable should be the ultimate goal.

REFERENCES

Centers for Medicare & Medicaid Services. 2002. *Healthcare Industry Update: Acute Care Hospitals.* Washington, DC: CMS, 27.

Collins, J. C. 2001. *Good to Great: Why Some Companies Make the Leap... and Others Don't*, 20, 39. New York: Harper Collins Publishers.

Collins, J. C., and J. I. Porras. 1996. "Building Your Company's Vision." *Harvard Business Review* September/October: 65

Drucker, P. F. 1999. *Innovation and Entrepreneurship*, 28. New York: HarperBusiness.

FedEx Corporation. 2003. "About Us." [Online information; retrieved 4/14/03.] http://www.fedex.com/us/about/corporation/awards.html.

Griffith, J. R. 2000. "Championship Management for Healthcare Organizations." *Journal of Healthcare Management* 45 (1): 17–30.

HP Services. 2000. "Customer Success: Starbucks Coffee Company." [Online information; retrieved 3/12/03.] http://h18005.www1.hp.com/services/success/stories/ss_starbucks.html.

Kohn, L., J. Corrigan, and M. Donaldson. 2000. *To Err is Human: Building a Safer Health System*. Washington DC: National Academy Press, Institute of Medicine.

Kaplan, R. S., and P. P. Norton. 1996. *Balanced Scorecard: Translating Strategy into Action*. Cambridge, MA: Harvard Business School Press.

National Commission on Entrepreneurship. 2001a. *Embracing Innovation: Entrepreneurship and American Economic Growth*. [Online information; retrieved 9/22/02.] http:// www.ncoe.org.

———. 2001b. *Five Myths About Entrepreneurs: Understanding How Businesses Start and Grow*" [Online information; retrieved 9/22/02.] http:// www.ncoe.org.

Porter, M. C. 1996. "What Is Strategy?" *Harvard Business Review* November/December: 77.

Starbucks.com. 2003. "Awards and Accolades." [Online information; retrieved 3/12/03.] http://www.starbucks.com/aboutus/recognition.asp.

About the Authors

Alan M. Zuckerman, FACHE, FAAHC, is a founding partner and director of Health Strategies & Solutions, Inc., a leading national healthcare consulting firm based in Philadelphia. Mr. Zuckerman has been a management consultant for 30 years, working exclusively for healthcare providers across the United States.

During his career, Mr. Zuckerman's consulting work has focused on strategic planning; this book is an outgrowth of his experience with hundreds of diverse healthcare organizations. Among his strategic planning clients have been large and small community hospitals, academic medical centers, single- and multispecialty physician groups, nursing homes, retirement centers, hospices, home care agencies, and psychiatric and rehabilitation specialty centers. In recent years, he has been involved in the development of increasingly sophisticated competitive strategies for leading hospitals, health systems, and academic medical centers.

Mr. Zuckerman is widely published and a frequent speaker at national healthcare conferences. His book *Healthcare Strategic Planning: Approaches for the 21st Century* won the 1999 American College of Healthcare Executives' James A. Hamilton book-of-the-year award. Mr. Zuckerman is a fellow of the American College of Healthcare Executives and of the American Association of Healthcare Consultants and a member of the Society for Healthcare Strategy and Market Development.

Russell C. Coile, Jr., is the editor of *Russ Coile's Health Trends* and senior strategist for Health Strategies & Solutions, Inc. He is a nationally recognized futurist who provides market forecasts and strategic advice to hospitals, medical groups, health plans, and suppliers on a nationwide basis. In 2002, he was ranked among the top 100 health leaders by *Modern Healthcare* magazine.

Mr. Coile is the author of ten books and numerous articles on the future of the health field. Since 2001, Mr. Coile has participated in over 100 seminars for groups including the American Hospital Association, the American College of Healthcare Executives, The Governance Institute, the American College of Physician Executives, and the Health Information and Management Systems Society.

Mr. Coile is the past president of the Society for Healthcare Strategy and Market Development of the American Hospital Association and a board member of the Center for Health Design and the Public Health Institute. He is also a member of editorial advisory boards, including *Managed Care Outlook, Nurse Week,* and *Healthcare Market Strategist.*